# THE WAY
## OF THE
# BODYPRAYERPATH

# THE WAY

## OF THE

## BODYPRAYERPATH

### Erotic Freedom and
### Spiritual Enlightenment

## Barnaby B. Barratt

To order additional copies of this book, contact:
Xlibris Corporation
1-888-795-4274
www.Xlibris.com
Orders@Xlibris.com
21064

# CONTENTS

*May all beings be happy and free;*
*May these writings contribute to the happiness*
*and freedom of all beings.*

# I

## "You are Invited . . ."

What is written here is both ancient and contemporary. These spiritual teachings are not new. Rather they are a new confluence of proven spiritual practices—many rivulets forming a powerful river that can carry us to the ocean of divine bliss. For heaven is available to every single one of us, right here and right now, on this earth. For the devoted practitioner of these teachings, the experience of heaven-on-earth is assured, and this is what is called our "spiritual enlightening."

The spiritual vision presented here is "tantric," which means that we are concerned with weaving and reweaving the sacred energies that are all around us and that lie within each of our sexual-spiritual bodies—waiting for us to awaken to them. We are concerned with releasing all that obstructs our potential for divine bliss, all that obstructs our capacity to live life in Love. We are invited onto the path of spiritual practices that facilitate our freedom to release ourselves into the flow of this powerful river.

This vision is tantric, and the oldest documented versions of tantric teaching come from the Hindu-Buddhist tradition. But they join together naturally with teachings from Taoist wisdom and from the Sufi inspiration of Islam, as well as from Kabbalistic Judaism, from Gnostic Christianity, and from many native traditions. In our hearts, we know that we are all one—we know that in our hearts pulses the lifeforce of one heart. We know that, as beautifully diverse as we are, we are all mere singular pulsations in the heartbeat of the entire universe. In our hearts, we all know

that the supreme flow of this universe is that of the truthfulness of
Love.

What this means will be discussed in these writings. We are
concerned here with processes that align our erotic being-in-the-
world with our hearts and with the supreme flow of the spiritual
universe. We are concerned with aligning our glorious genitals,
our minds and our hearts by releasing ourselves from the egotism
of our chattering minds. By "our glorious genitals" we refer to the
miraculous blessings of all our sensuality, the ecstatic potential of
our sexual body, and the erotic sensitivities of our natural
embodiment as human beings. By "our chattering minds" we refer
to our business and our busyness. We refer to our chattering
consciousness to mean all the incessant thoughts about what was
or what will be, that all too readily govern our lives—all the beliefs,
doctrines and dogma that tend to preoccupy us when we live "in
our heads." Letting go these preoccupations, tantric spiritual
practice concerns living with what *is* here-and-now, experiencing
this present life to the fullest, and enjoying—finding joy in—the
energies of our erotic embodiment. Finding our bliss, surrendering
to the flow of the universe, aligning our sexual energies with our
hearts and so too with the rhythm of the heavens, is the spiritual
practice of the *"bodyprayerpath."* It is simply a matter of allowing
what is already here-and-now to manifest itself, a matter of allowing
heaven to manifest on this present earth.

You are invited to amuse yourself with what is written here. To
allow what is written to evoke the calling of your energies and your
heart, to allow yourself to play with these words. For what is written
here is not a matter for debate. Our chattering minds can readily
"disprove"—and thus entirely mistake—the blessings of spiritual
experiences that are already long since proven. Heaven is here,
even amidst the desecrations wrought by the human mind. The
call of the heart, the enticement of joyful spiritual practice, is
ultimately unmistakable.

# II

## Living in "Hell"

It is not difficult to imagine that we are living in hell. For most of us, much of the time, life is indeed hellish. Let's face it: Our lives are full of suffering.

Indeed, the opportunity to suffer emotionally and physically presents itself at every twist and turn of our life's course. Disasters affect our material welfare. We deteriorate or become damaged through the course of life's events. Disturbance and distress often characterize our relationships with others, both with those whom we "love" and with those who might be considered our "enemies." In one way or another, suffering is everywhere, and affects everyone.

Sooner or later, we all experience crisis and tragedy. Not only are violence, warfare, injustice, impoverishment, and ecological suicide all around us. But we are also traumatized in each of our private lives. Our best intentions, our elaborate ambitions, our dearest attachments, and our most fervent dreams, sooner or later come to naught. At each phase of our lives, every one of us experiences loss, often profound or catastrophic loss. And, although we like to delude ourselves that this is not the case, everything we appear to create—from "love affairs" to lifelong friendships, from tall towers to "timeless thoughts," from books to bank accounts, from dreams to destinies—will eventually be destroyed. We all face the inevitability of aging, disease, disability, destruction and death.

But what is inevitable about this, and is suffering really inevitable? Does life have to be hellish, or do we, as humans, have an awful ability to make life hellish, both for ourselves and for others? Let us consider the "causes" of our suffering, both those that are avoidable, and those that appear to be unavoidable. We shall see here that many of life's hardships are avoidable. Their occurrence is a result of the malicious ways in which we humans think, feel or act, and whether we suffer in reaction to their occurrence is very much a production of the human mind. Many of life's hardships are unavoidable—for example, every human being faces pain and loss in the course of life. But whether we suffer as a result of pain and loss is very much a question of our "mental attitude," or—more precisely—it is a matter of our spiritual grounding.

Clearly, many of what appear to be the "causes" of our suffering are not inevitable. They are the production of the human mind. Humans are continually going to war with each other, yet warfare is not necessary. Wars are avoidable, were it not for the malice of the human mind. In fact, as a species, humans are quite distinctive for our persistent inclination to fight, torture, and kill each other. Plants and animals certainly both cooperate and compete with each other, engaging in a complex cycle wherein the destruction of some permits the creation of others. Yet plants and animals scarcely show "hatred" for each other as each takes its place in the ecological complex. The human capacity for hatred is distinct. We fight, torture, and kill, even though our material and spiritual needs could be met without the destruction of our own brethren. All this is not caused by physical necessity. Rather, we are, as a species, emotionally addicted to an excess of violence.

Clearly, injustice and impoverishment are also not inevitable. There is no necessary reason why the few oppress the many. No unalterable reason why the world is ruled by robber barons. No unavoidable reason why, all over the world, children, women, and minorities are mistreated and abused. No inescapable reason why everyday the majority of humans face malnutrition, toxicity, prejudice and poor living conditions. None of this is inevitable. Rather, it is endemic to the way in which we humans think, feel, and act.

This wonderful planet is abundant, but neither inexhaustible nor indestructible. It has offered us the opportunity to enjoy more than enough food and shelter, as well as untold beauties and hidden delights. It offers this abundance to a human community—to one that is not hell bent on aggrandizing itself, believing itself to be sovereign, and committing itself to the greedy desecration of the earth's resources. Despite this plenitude, as humans we are rapidly destroying the ecological viability of the planet. We have poisoned the earth, the seas, and the skies. We have plundered and trashed our own home. We take more than we give. We try to possess what we cannot. We accumulate more than we need. And we have become a cancer on the planet.

Clearly, there has been nothing inevitable about our violence, warfare, injustice, and impoverishment, or our evident commitment to ecological suicide. These nightmares are distinctively the production of human thought, feeling, and action.

We may notice here how much we are accustomed to blame others. Rarely is it "me" who acknowledges doing these awful deeds. Usually the "other" person starts the war, making it "regretfully necessary" that we fight. Or we convince ourselves that the other somehow "deserves" to be tortured, maimed or maltreated, because the other is inferior to us and "bad." We convince ourselves that the other person is so different from us, yet fundamentally all human minds chatter alike. Our chattering mind is committed to strategies of domination. We insist that our life is more important than the lives of others, our greed more important than the sanctity of the planet. We insist that we are "better" than others. We subjugate children. We subordinate women and minorities. We denigrate and persecute those who are "different" in any way. When we can, we lord ourselves over any other person or thing, just so that we can feel that we are "better." Just so that we can prove how right it is to be us. Just so that we can aggrandize ourselves, as if we were truly powerful and sufficient unto ourselves. Just so that we can delude ourselves that we will never die. These ambitions of our chattering mind are indeed the cause of much human misery. Through such ambitions of human thought, feeling, and action, the circumstances for violence, warfare, injustice, impoverishment, and ecological suicide are perpetually created.

Clearly, there are also many "causes" of our suffering that do indeed appear to be inevitable. Beyond all the hardship and hatred that we humans inflict on each other, there is hardship that is inherent to life itself. Life inevitably involves the hurtfulness and the harshness of pain and loss. These are aspects of everyone's personal journey. Bonds of "love" and hate attach us to others, yet sooner or later we lose every relationship we have. Everything and everyone that is dear to us is eventually lost. In our personal journey, we all encounter decay, disease, and death. Our egotism strives to assert that this "me" is certain of itself, secure within itself, powerful and perhaps everlasting, yet sooner or later we lose every aspect of ourselves that we ever valued. None of this is avoidable. Our lives are often extremely painful. It is inherent to the process of life itself.

Yet how much we suffer from these experiences of hardship, pain and loss depends very much on our spiritual "attitude" or orientation toward them. Our tears of sadness in the face of these experiences are very natural, and indeed necessary for our spiritual healing and growth. Yet, in a crucial sense, our suffering as a result of these experiences is a product of the way in which we humans think, feel, and act. Suffering is a production of our chattering mind. It is the chattering mind that produces our hopes and expectations for what it imagines to be perfection; our hopes and expectations for relationships that would last forever; our hopes and expectations for a life without pain or loss; and our delusion that somehow we might never die. It is these hopes and expectations that are the cause of our suffering.

Let us not misunderstand what is written here. The tragedy of being human—the misery we inflict on each other, the despotic way we have treated the planet, and the inescapable misery of decay, disease, and death—is not a matter for indifference. It is only ethical to refuse to participate in our own propensity for violence, warfare, injustice, impoverishment, and ecological desecration. It is only ethical to offer our efforts toward alleviating the misery of hardship, pain and loss. It is only ethical to shed our tears of sadness, and to bring joy into our own lives as well as the lives of all other beings.

The ethical, existential and experiential path is that of spiritual healing, starting here-and-now, each of us within ourselves. Although it certainly could eliminate our predilection for violence, warfare, injustice, impoverishment, and ecological desecration, healing is not an eradication of the trauma and tragedy of being human. That is not possible, for hardship, pain and loss are inherent to life itself. Rather, spiritual healing concerns how we experience our encounters with pain and loss, how we experience all that is hurtful and harsh. Simply stated, healing concerns whether we experience life's trauma and tragedy with suffering or with serenity, whether we choose misery or joy.

Humanity today is in a fearful, frightening mess. The anguish of being human is everywhere apparent. No doubt it has always been so. But today we face not only the nightmare of miseries that humans inflict on each other; we face the imminent destruction of the planet. This is the apotheosis of the human mind as it chatters away, in a futile effort to make itself supreme, forever or even for a day.

Each of us specifically, and humanity in general, desperately needs spiritual practice. Because only through spiritual practice will the chattering mind give way to the heart; and, only through spiritual practice, will the exuberant, joyous lifeforce that flows all around us be celebrated within our embodiment. But, here is the surprise that is no surprise. Here is the secret suppressed and repressed within us, the secret that is repeatedly censored and oppressed by the calamitous forces of what is sometimes, absurdly, called "civilization." The practice of spiritual healing, turning suffering into serenity, and hell into heaven, is erotic. It involves, for each of us, our living, breathing, dancing, moving, vibrating, orgasming, lovemaking bodymind. It involves the sensuality of our sexual bodies and the alignment of our erotic lifeforce with the magnificence of our heart.

It is our fearfulness of the erotic lifeforce within us that fuels our human propensity for aggression, exploitation, and hatred. This fearfulness renders us alienated within ourselves. Emotionally, this fearfulness causes our attachment to the malicious judgmentalism of the chattering mind by which, in condemning ourselves and others, we perpetuate our own suffering as well as the suffering of all those around us and of the planet itself. All this, precisely because we have become spiritually separated from the erotic sourcing within us. All this, precisely because we live in alienation, and not in meditation. All this, precisely because our thoughts, feelings and actions operate on the basis of our fear of the sexual-spiritual lifeforce that undulates within and through our bodies.

Suffering is a spiritual condition. It is the result of our alienation from our own spiritual sourcing. Health, healing, and happiness are available to each and every one of us, even while life is hurtful and harsh. For it is our chattering mind that makes life hellish— even while it tells us incessantly that it is only trying to serve us by seeking our "just reward," by establishing our self-righteousness, by securing our invulnerability, and perhaps even by guaranteeing our eternal life. Only as we release ourselves from our imprisonment within these deluded ambitions, only as we release ourselves from the hollow grandeur of our chattering mind, can we become truly and serenely alive. And as we become truly alive, we find the joy in all of life, including all that is hurtful and harsh. We give ourselves over to heaven-on-earth. We surrender our egotism, and experience the divinity that is within. There is Holy Spirit within each of us. Only spiritual practices that embrace this erotic lifeforce can free us from our suffering. Our sexual freeing is the path of spiritual enlightening.

# III

## Reality and Ecstatic Emptiness

What is reality? We all like to think that we know it, that it is "out there," solid and substantial—as reliable as the table at which we sit, as beautiful as a blossoming tree, as horrendous as the face of a maimed and starving child. Our everyday unreflective consciousness believes that reality simply is, out there, waiting for us to experience it, waiting for us to react to it with our thoughts, our feelings, and our actions. And in a certain sense, all this may be correct. But in a more profound sense, life is far more complexly mysterious than this reality grasped by our unawakened consciousness.

If we look more deeply into these matters, we realize how much we expend our lives living in fantasy; how much our unawakened consciousness compels us to dwell in fabricated realities of a deluded design that we call our own; how much our lives are conditioned and constrained by the stories that are told and retold within the society or culture we are born into; how much we live, not in the presence of our immediate existence, here-and-now, but rather in the past history of all our stories about what has been experienced before, or in the future expectation of all our stories about what experiences will await us ahead.

Our chattering mind incessantly peddles stories about our experience, as if insisting that we must live in beliefs about what we are now experiencing. We conduct our lives in the "reality" of what are called "belief systems"—an edifice of thoughts, feelings and actions that give us a misleading sense of what is "really real." Belief systems are sets of stories told and retold within our sociocultural context—stories that we have come to adopt, and to which we are dearly attached. We think, feel and act in the world through such stories.

Even our experience of mundane objects, such as a tree or a table, are conditioned and constrained by the narrative forms of story-telling convention. This table may just seem to be here, a substantial reality independent of any human consciousness, but our experience of it requires a confabulation of narratives about tables, beliefs about what a table is, and beliefs about how tables may be experienced. We do not have direct access to the "reality" of a particular tree standing there in front of us, for this tree is only experienced within a network of meanings that we bring to it, a history of stories about other trees we have experienced, and about ourselves in relation to such matters.

Our minds operate in systems of meaning that are almost entirely closed. The everyday reality we live in is a represented reality—and, in an important sense, everything that can be represented has already been represented. It is *re*-presented, and anything "new" will have to conform to the rules of representation. That is, it will have to be represent-able, or our mind will not be able to believe that it really exists. Our chattering mind attempts to enclose our experience, keeping us living in our stories about the past and the future.

Our mind's enclosure also operates in relation to ideas as well as mundane objects. We know well that, when facing a maimed and starving child, different people have different reactions. Some will be horrified; some will deny their horror; some will not be horrified. Some will express outrage; some would prefer to kill the child rather than tolerate the excruciating feelings the child evokes. Some will frantically perform acts of charity; some will relish the fact that such a fate has befallen that child, rather than themselves or a child of their own. Some believe they "know" that this child must be being punished by a judgmental god; others believe they "know" that the child is conclusive proof that Love is not to be found in this world. Typically, whatever our reaction to this situation, we are convinced of the rightness of how we think, feel or act, and are usually ready to judge other reactions as incomprehensible or merely "wrong."

Our chattering mind attempts to govern our life mythematically— by myths and themes—and moralistically. We are full of ideas about what life "really is about," even while these ideas and beliefs actually obstruct our experience of life itself. We fortify ourselves with the "rightness" of our beliefs. Our chattering mind tells us that life only "makes sense" if we believe, for example, that "family values should be cherished," that "sodomy is immoral," or that "this is God's country like none other." Our chattering minds are cluttered with such beliefs, incessantly repeating them in a stream of endless chatter. Such is the fantasy world that our unawakened consciousness causes us to inhabit.

We hold all these representations as if they are "really real"— rather than merely being *re*-presentations. We need to believe in the solid "reality" of trees and tables; we are sure our life would fall apart if it were not for the "reality" constructed by our social values, our moralizing tenets, and our religious faiths. But the force of our convictions lies mostly in the frequency with which these representations of "reality" are compulsively repeated by our chattering minds. Notice that if we repeat any nonsensical statement long enough, it will become "meaningful." It may become our absolute truth, to which we believe we ourselves, as well as everyone else, should adhere. Or it may become an absolute lie, which we are indignant to think those other—bad, stupid, immoral—people actually believe. But either way, the repetition has made the statement into a significant proposition that now governs our lives and our experience of life.

Perhaps the most elaborated and spiritually dangerous set of stories for each of us is that surrounding the representation of "me." Each of these representations is, like all representations, a duality, because it is always bound to a contingent and contrasting set of representations about everything that is "not-me." This me/not-me complex is actually a sociocultural construction, given to us from outside ourselves and then adopted as our own. Each of us likes to think that we author these stories, and that we are each the master of our own—represented—experiences. But in a more profound sense, we are the product of the narrative systems into which we are born, and in which we are embedded. For each of us, there were stories about this "me" even before we were born into the world. For example, our parents had elaborate fantasy systems, both conscious and unconscious, about what we would become; the sociocultural structures and organizations around us determined what would be possible for us to do, and how we could grow into this world. Complex fantasy systems make up the sociocultural network into which we are born, and into which we are socialized and acculturated. These fantasy systems are beliefs about the world, about human relationships, and about the possibilities of our personhood. They are both conscious, in the sense that they can be articulated upon inquiry, and unconscious, in the sense that their meanings are suppressed or repressed, their operation being unrecognized by those who participate in their content. Unconscious fantasy systems are especially powerful in determining who we think we are, and what we do. So in large measure, we are told who we are, what we are, and how we are to experience our world and ourselves. In the context of these sociocultural processes, the "individuality" of our chattering mind is constructed. It is far from individually unique. Rather, for all of us, it is an inauthentic pastiche, composed almost entirely of chatter taken from the airwaves around us.

As we develop from infancy to adulthood, our chattering mind is preoccupied with the distinction between "good" and "bad"—along with a medley of associated attributions such as pleasing/not-pleasing, right/wrong, and normal/abnormal. The duality of good/bad precedes and goes along with the elaborated construction of me/not-me. In this manner, we learn to position ourselves in the world, as we represent it, by the compulsively repetitious enunciation of decisions. To "decide" means to separate and to evaluate or judge. To separate, as in "this is me, and that is not-me," and then to judge, as in "this is good, and that is bad." And to our chattering mind, "good" means whatever supports "me," whatever aggrandizes the chattering mind, whatever appears to make "me" dominant, whatever appears to make me king of all that is, whatever appears to ensure the immortality of my egotism. Our chattering mind chatters precisely to secure, stabilize and substantiate this pastiche of "me." This medley of judgmental chatter is how we exist when we are not spiritually awakened. It has been called self, ego, personality, or mundane consciousness, but we will call it the "egotism" of the chattering mind. It is compulsively repetitious, incessantly judgmental, perpetually inauthentic, and pervasively deluded. As we will come to understand, our egotism is what obstructs our access to the erotic sourcing of Holy Spirit within us, and it is the origin of all human malice. The egotism of our chattering mind is what renders us aggressive, exploitive, hateful, and suicidal. It imprisons us by choking our access to the lifeforce that is all around us and within us, and it leads us into attachments of bondage, to which it often gives the name of "love."

Clearly, what we commonly think of as "reality" is not what we imagine it is. What our unawakened consciousness calls "reality" is an enormously cumbersome edifice of thoughts, feelings and actions that is propped up only by the incessant and compulsive repetition of its contents. Our chattering mind has us living in fantasy, for the egotistic condition of human cognition is the systematic construction of deludedness. This is a vast edifice of attachments: relationships of "love" and hate, belief systems, doctrines and dogmas, ideologies, myths and themes. It is the edifice within which we live, unawakened, as we go about our mundane lives. We live in a dream—more accurately a nightmare— of human construction. We suffer endlessly because of our attachment to all these ideologies, stories, and systems of belief. We suffer because of our egotism, because of the incessant judgmentalism of our chattering mind.

So what is "reality"? What truly is behind, beneath and beyond this edifice of our beliefs, stories, and ideologies? What existence or experience might be available to us, calling us in some way that is otherwise than our attachments? Contemporary philosophy deconstructs human cognition, showing that there is no absolute foundation to the logical and rhetorical forum of our thoughts, feelings and actions. All such matters are relative and ultimately insecure. The deconstructive practice of psychoanalysis demonstrates how our attachment to conscious and unconscious beliefs merely serves our egotism by obstructing the free-flow of exuberant energies within our sexual-spiritual body. Other sciences show us: that the substantial form of things, from tables to trees, is merely an accretion of energies; that the forms of thought, feeling and action are also merely energetic configurations; and that the entire universe itself is a nonlinear complex of interdependent energies that sometimes coagulate into transient forms and sometimes release themselves into the flow of existence.

What is implied by these scientific findings is that whenever something is "present" as re-presented, it is always already absent; whatever can be manifested is charged by the energies of all that remains immanifest, and that cannot be manifested. The representation of here-and-now is always already there-and-then; the representational world of our chattering mind cannot open itself to the authentic presence of the here-and-now for this presence is a vortex. Our egotism's attachment to representation means that we prevent ourselves from experiencing the present. Rather, we live in an absent past and an absent future. Our egotism's preoccupation with all our thoughts, feelings and actions—its compulsively repetitious need to make decisions, to establish the me/not-me and evaluate good/bad—obstructs the spiritual truthfulness of our experiencing. This repetitious chatter blocks our access to the presenting absence and the absenting presence. The edifice of our egotism obscures our experience of the divine energies that are all around us, and the divine energies that are within.

Ancient practices of meditation intimate how, as soon as we release ourselves from the repetitive chatter of our thoughts, feelings and actions, we find ourselves surrendering to a deep aliveness, an energy of silence that is within. In this spiritual practice, we realize existentially and experientially that underneath the edifice of our beliefs, stories and ideologies is an ecstatic emptiness, a blissful flow of sacred energies. The truthfulness of reality—what is *really real*—is the Sacred Unity of all being and nonbeing, which is this ecstatic emptiness that pervades and eludes all our deluded representations about life.

In spiritual practice, we realize how bliss is accessible and abundantly available to us, as we release ourselves from the imprisonment of our chattering mind. In spiritual practice, we surrender to the flow of being-nonbeing that is this ecstatic emptiness. We realize that this ecstatic emptiness is the Sacred Unity of all being and nonbeing. We realize that this Sacred Unity is the supreme flow of the energies of the universe, which is here-and-now in every moment of our existence, but which is beyond our chattering mind's capacity to comprehend. And we realize blissfully that this Sacred Unity of ecstatic emptiness is the absolute truthfulness of Love.

# IV

## The Erotic Calling of our Holy Spirit

When "He" or "She" endowed us with an abundance of sexual energies, surely "God's" intention was to empower our spiritual growth, to offer us the most powerful way by which we may deconstruct our egotism. Because our egotism is the very aspect of our humanity that keeps us from realizing our union with the divine.

Contrary to the mistaken teaching that sexual energy precipitates our spiritual downfall, our sexuality is the divine blessing of an embodied spirit. It is the power by which we may realize our spiritual calling, which is to live heaven-on-earth. "God" gave us sexual energies as the flow of the lifeforce into which we may choose to surrender our egotism; to dislodge our rational-cognitive fixations; to loosen the persistent repetition-compulsiveness of our chattering minds; to let go the attachments of our own deludedness; to awaken spiritually by opening ourselves to the joyous vibrancy of the universe's grace.

As soon as the attachments and preoccupations of our chattering mind are relinquished, we realize how the universe is a flowing emptiness of energy, the pure light of Love. This energy is vibrant yet intensely still, ecstatically exuberant yet silent. It permeates all things and all events, yet is incomprehensible. It is the timespace of all joy, ecstasy and bliss. This emptiness of the Sacred Unity, which is the lifeforce and the light of Love, is eternal. It is the only One that is non-contingent, infinite and everlasting—whereas all the phenomena to which it gives life are interdependent, impermanent, and subject to the cycling of creation and destruction.

Sacred energies flow all around us in ways that are almost entirely mysterious. These esoteric energies are available to our existence, accessible to our spiritual experience, yet neither thinkable nor sayable, and not measurable in any manner such that our chattering mind could accept them as "irrefutable fact." Our mind thinks it knows a lot about the functioning of certain levels of energy. We can point to theories about how waves become particles, and particles dissolve into waves. Sciences, from astronomy to psychology and microbiology, teach us how to assess and evaluate all sorts of transformations caused by energies. We can measure some of what occurs anatomically and physiologically within the human body; we can even measure energy changes in the neuronal cortex concomitant with altered states of consciousness. But for all this skillful knowledge, esoteric teachings tell us that what is measurable in this manner is comparatively gross. Spiritual practice still points to dimensions of energy too subtle for conventional science to comprehend. The sacred energies of life remain mysterious.

Our sexuality is ultimately mysterious. It is the door to life's deepest wonder. Conventional science has not grasped, and cannot comprehend, the esoteric dimension of our erotic potential. Western sexology—the science of sexuality—tends to define human sexuality as a specific repertoire of behaviors that are called "sexual," as the gross physiological responses that can be recorded during arousal and orgasm, or as the system of conscious and unconscious fantasies that accompany the individual's erotic excitement. Such definitions miss the key spiritual dimension of human sexuality: Sexuality is the movement of subtle energies within and through our erotic embodiment. In this sense, our sexuality is the spiritual dimension of being human. Although taking our experience beyond our cognitive capacity, these erotic energies are always accessible to us, whatever our bodily condition, and however much our chattering mind strives to block or freeze them into immobilized congestion.

As soon as we become spiritually aware, we realize to our immense joy that erotic energies are everywhere around us—in the swaying dance of the blossoming tree, in the shimmering particles that hold themselves together as a table, in all the creative beauty of nature as well as in its awesome destructive power. And yes, erotic energies are also there in the sickbed, in the torture chamber, and in the crematorium. As Kabbalist mystics such as Isaac Luria teach us, sparks of holiness are mingled within everything that is in the world. And their living presence in every cell of our erotic embodiment is the here-and-now of our spiritual calling.

Our human embodiment, from the cradle to the grave, harbors an abundance of erotic energies. We are a temporary container for this lifeforce that pulsates within us. For some, being a "temporary container" seems like a negligible matter, but such is the talk of the chattering mind with its egotistic ambition and phony grandeur. For those who are spiritually awakened, there could not be a more miraculous blessing. To be a conduit for the momentum of the divine, to be aware of the erotic lifeforce that undulates within and through our embodiment, is the sourcing of all joy, ecstasy and bliss.

Although we are fearful and traumatized such that erotic energies become obstructed or immobilized by our egotism—giving rise to our compulsively repetitious edifice of chattering thoughts, feelings and actions, as well as to our psychosomatic blockages—every cell of our embodiment is still a miraculous conduit for the energies of the lifeforce. Every fiber of our being pulsates with erotic energies. We are intrinsically erotic, from head to toe. We are blessed with an incredible "polysexual" potential for sensual enjoyment. Our capacity for erotic joy is ubiquitous and diverse. We are a living miracle.

Our embodiment is miraculous, in pleasure and in pain, whatever judgments we hold about its condition. The sexual-spiritual potential of our embodiment is not just for those whom society designates as "attractive," or "youthful," or "physically fit." Erotic freedom and spiritual enlightening are available to all. For we all can experience the undulating flow of the Holy Spirit arising within us, vibrating through our being, aligning us with heaven-on-earth.

Our erotic potential is our access to Holy Spirit. We note that this potential is "polysexual" because the spiritual dimension of sexuality is to be found in everything erotic, and our capacity to find erotic enjoyment is, for each and every one of us, extraordinarily and enigmatically diverse. Although the streaming of erotic energies up from our pelvic root to our crown is most dramatic, we are all capable of orgasming just in our little finger, our armpit, our perineum. And yes, after our chattering mind has subsided, we are even capable of orgasming just "in our mind." Moreover, our capacity for erotic enjoyment is, for each and every one of us, not an individual matter, and not to be partitioned or compartmentalized. All of us may practice our sexuality in every way. There is no manner of sexual expression that is "not for us," for we are all polysexual and "pan-erotic." We may practice our sexuality solo, or with all sorts of human partners, and we may practice our sexuality with the beauty of trees or in the awesome surrounds of a graveyard. We may practice our sexuality in this way or in that, for there is no "right" or "wrong" pertinent here. But, however we practice, our erotic enjoyment implicates the entire universe, because we are all, and everything is, deeply connected in a nonlinear interdependent way, and every movement of erotic energies may further the joy of the cosmos. In this sense, "lovemaking"—accessing the Love that energizes the universe and that casts our egotism into ecstatic emptiness—is always a sacred calling, always a momentum that has the potential to align our humanity with the divine Sacred Unity that embraces all.

Our erotic energy *is* Holy Spirit, vibrating around, within and through the being of our bodymind. Our "libido," our "kundalini" energies, or our *prāna*—our erotic lifeforce—is our access to the divine. Our sexualities beckon us onto the spiritual path; our sexualities are the gateway to our divinity; our sexualities are the manifestation of our Holy Spirit. Only the energy of our sexualities has the power to invite our egotism into its blissful dissolution.

And this is why, only through the freeing of our sexualities, can we surrender to the Sacred Unity that embraces all.

The erotic calling of our sensual vitality offers us choices in every moment of our life's course. Do we spend our life inviting our egotism to step aside, making way for the flow of divine energy within, or do we expend our life bolstering our egotism, pursuing all sorts of futile ambitions, and struggling to suppress or repress the erotic exuberance that is within? Are we to devote our lives surrendering into *being* divine light, or are we to squander our lives *doing* all sorts of egotistically important things, concocting legacies that will become dust in the wind?

Our erotic calling entices us to dance sexually-spiritually through life. Our egotism demands that we stand fearfully frozen in the repetitive preoccupations of our chattering mind. Our erotic calling invites us to accede to the grace of the Sacred Unity that nourishes all, to surrender ourselves to the ecstatic emptiness that envelops and permeates all being and nonbeing. Our egotism bribes us to refine our ambitions, accumulate social successes, and leave our mark on the world. Our erotic calling offers us a life of grace— celebrating the joy of living—a life lived in compassion and appreciation for whatever is. Our egotism insists that we inhabit only what is past and future, dwelling in our deludedness, and ultimately facing our death with nothing more than a sense of horror.

Our erotic energies provide the way to experience the Sacred Unity of the divine. Our erotic nature calls us toward the ecstatic emptiness that is within all things. Our erotic energies are the secret to finding the joy in all things and in every eventuality. Yet to follow this path, to surrender ourselves to the secret of this calling, intimates the termination of our egotism. The sexual-spiritual calling of Holy Spirit within us is what our chattering mind chatters against. We are embarked on the path that our egotism finds more frightening than anything imaginable. It is precisely our egotism's terror of our erotic potential that is the root of all human malice.

# V

## The Origins of Malice

The Holy Spirit within us is the supreme gift and our supreme challenge. Flowing all around, within and through us, our erotic energy *is* Holy Spirit. It calls us to our spiritual life. It challenges us to live life in Love, to surrender ourselves to the vibrationality of ecstatic emptiness, to live in our hearts and our sexual bodies, and to liberate ourselves from the malicious preoccupations of our chattering mind. All this spells catastrophe for our egotism.

It is often said that the reason we humans think, feel and act is to ensure our wellbeing—to enable us to be well fed, well hydrated, well protected from climatic extremes, and well nourished by our relatedness with others. In a very limited sense, this may be partially correct. But in a more profound sense, it is crucially mistaken. If individual survival or communal wellbeing were its purpose, it is obvious that most of the chattering mind's activities are entirely superfluous, if not deleterious. If species survival were its purpose, it is obvious that most of the chattering mind's activities are entirely sabotaging of any hope of achieving its own goal. No!—The human mind, in its chattering consciousness, is not interested in our health, our healing, or even ultimately our happiness. This mode of consciousness, which is our egotism, is only interested in maintaining and advancing itself. Any concern it may appear to show for our individual or communal wellbeing is derived from our egotism's ambition for dominion. Our egotism is only interested in its own perpetuation—its own security, stability, and sense of unique significance—its own bloatedness.

Our egotism is founded on fearfulness. At its foundations, this is not so much a fear of our failing to survive, individually or communally. Rather, our egotism is founded on its fearful ambition to protect its own constructions. The greatest threat to our egotism does not come from our being unhealthy, unhealed, or unhappy. Actually, our egotism ensures that this is our condition—even while it chatters about how it wants only the best for us. The greatest threat to our egotism comes from the erotic *deathfulness* of our human bodymind, a deathfulness that pervades its own constructions. This deathfulness *is* the flowing existence of the here-and-now. It is the deathfulness that is present in the sexual-spiritual momentum of our embodiment. It is the deathfulness that celebrates itself in our orgasming. This deathfulness is our Holy Spirit casting us into ecstatic emptiness.

Why do we turn away from Holy Spirit within us? Opening ourselves to the energies of the divine immediately reveals the hollow grandeur of our egotistic ambitions. To open ourselves to the flowing energies of ecstatic emptiness is to reveal that the solidity, stability or surety of our "present reality," as *re*-presented by our chattering mind, is actually an abyss. *Deathfulness* is inherent and integral to every moment of life itself. Our egotism founds itself on its fearfulness of this momentum, its fearfulness of the liveliness of life itself.

Our chattering mind systematically deceives us by considering death in only one or two ways. It acknowledges death as the conclusion of our life's narrative, the end of our personhood and the terminus toward which our life is unavoidably set. Death is the point at which the body ceases to breathe, its living functions cease, and its remains are fit only for disposal. From our egotism's standpoint, this sort of death is acknowledged, even though it finds such a termination quite incomprehensible, and definitely unacceptable or undesirable. The body, which our egotism views as if it were its slave, may desist, but our egotism insists that our egotism itself should keep on going. So it invents narratives of "immortal accomplishment," of "making my mark on the world," of being "remembered forever," and of life-after-death. But in all of this, our egotism senses the imminence of its own annihilation. We all grow up experiencing traumatization that intimates the annihilation of our egotism. A traumatization is any event in which the capacity of our chattering mind to believe that it is in control of life is dramatically and terrifyingly interrupted. Our egotism has these intimations of its own annihilation, and it is hell-bent on never allowing such an eventuality to occur again. Better to invent the delusion of its own life-after-death and better to expend the course of life bolstering itself, than to realize and enjoy—find the joy in—the erotic deathfulness of life itself.

Deathfulness resides in every moment of life itself. Just as each moment of presence brings an absencing, and everything present manifests all that is absent, absence is inherent and integral in the presentness of the present. Our egotism is built precisely to ward off our experience of this deathfulness of all that exists and so—against this potential for sexual-spiritual awakening—it promulgates its own beliefs that it might be king, by anxiously constructing an ideological edifice of grand design. The grander the design, the more our egotism blinds itself to the reality of its own irreparable inadequacy and insufficiency.

Our egotism lives as if what it most wants to avoid is the realization that "despite the magnitude of my ambitions, I can never master any aspect of my own life's narrative, and my chattering mind will never be king despite its pretensions and its propensity for peddling grandiose delusions." What our egotism wants to avoid is the dual realization, the reality, both of what has been called its own intrinsic "castratedness"—by which we mean its irreparable inadequacy and insufficiency—and of what we are calling the inherent "deathfulness" of what it represents as life itself. Our egotism is terrified of realizing the impossibility of its own ambition to be master. It founds itself on its fear of realizing the truthfulness of life's impermanence. It builds its edifice on the deluded assumption that perhaps the entities in our life will not all be lost, perhaps there is something invincible about "me" and "my" judgmentalism.

Yet inevitably, accomplishments fade, relationships end, everything deteriorates or decays, meaninglessness installs itself, and every one of the beliefs or stories our egotism establishes about ourselves terminates in death. Deathfulness is everywhere within and around us, and our erotic potential is its harbinger.

For the edifice of our egotism, the potential power of our unbridled erotic energies is the greatest of all dangers, for here is lifeforce far greater than our egotism. Here is a power that our egotism cannot eradicate and ultimately cannot even control. This is why, for all of us, our sensual and sexual embodiment is—in some way or other—the locus of anxiety and conflict for our chattering mind. This is why, for each and every human being, our sexuality—in one way or another—always bears the traces of our egotism's shame and guilt about its expression. Our chattering mind burdens all of us with its fearfulness of our erotic potential, its terror of the one power whose freedom would dissolve our egotism into the oblivion of our bliss.

Yet this potential, our sexual-spiritual sourcing, persistently intimates the deathfulness of our representations. Our egotism is founded precisely as an anti-erotic force, against the sexual-spiritual momentum of its own dissolution. Our life's narratives function to suppress or repress our erotic exuberance, and thus the function of our chattering mind's incessant judgmentalism is precisely to attenuate or obstruct the joy we may find in the energies of our erotic embodiment.

Psychoanalysis offers us a wealth of information about this functioning: how our egotism develops itself by suppression and repression of the lifeforce within us; how egotism constructs its edifice by plundering the erotic joys of our embodiment, blocking and perverting our sensual energies for the purposes of its own production; how our sexual expression comes to be imbued with our chattering mind's production of shame and guilt; and how this "mind" is antagonistic to the wisdom of our "body," attempting to enslave it.

Some of the strategies deployed in our egotism's agenda are as follows: Our egotism may suppress, repress, or inhibit our sexual-spiritual energies—rendering them as if they were unavailable to our awareness. It may segregate or channelize them—as if licensing some limited and attenuated forms of sexual expression in order to attenuate or control the overall exuberance of our erotic potential. It may reinforce these strategies by attributing its own suppressed, repressed, or inhibited inclinations to some "other" person or entity, which it can then condemn and attack with its judgmentalism. It may attempt to turn sensual expression into something else that accords with its own ambitions—as if deploying one or more of these strategies to transmute erotic energy into forces of its own anti-sexual preoccupations. And our egotism may indulge in "sex" precisely to avoid the reality, power and exuberance of our erotic potential—as when "sex" becomes abusive, compulsive, or phobic and avoidant, and what is called "sex" actually becomes anti-sexual.

All these strategies, in which the sexual-spiritual potential of our erotic embodiment is diverted by our egotism, are performed by the judgmentalism of our chattering mind. Judgmentalism is our egotism's "modus operandi," and we need to understand this more deeply.

We humans are blessed with mental faculties and competences. We need—and are grateful—to be able to distinguish heat and cold, to know when there is hunger or thirst to be addressed, to be able to discern and learn. Such abilities are beautiful. They are necessary to the conduct of our life, including its sexual-spiritual path, for they support our wellbeing and our awareness of life itself. However, judgmentalism subverts these intentions, misappropriating our mental abilities for its own ends. Judgmentalism is what trips us away from our sexual-spiritual path, taking us out of the awareness of our erotic embodiment, making us live in the representations of past and future, and obscuring the presence and presentness of our authentic experience.

Against the awareness of our sexual-spiritual sourcing, the chattering mind perpetually and repetitiously preoccupies us with judgmental activities, incessantly pronouncing its decisions as to what is "good" and what is "bad," what is superior/inferior, forceful/weak, right/wrong, normal/abnormal, and so on. Such pronouncements inflate our egotism in various ways.

Judgmentalism divides the world into either/or—it makes decisions that both separate and categorize matters into a hierarchy of dichotomies. In the here-and-now of our authentic experience, nothing is really either/or, nothing is so separated—not even pleasure and pain. Yet our egotism insists on cutting the world into the binary constructions of decision-making, because it cannot tolerate the fluidity of ecstatic energy that suffuses and subverses its own edifice. The chattering mind has to keep on making its pronouncements lest it be swept into the stillness of its own deepest emptiness. To bolster itself, our egotism has to judge incessantly, even when it acknowledges that there is nothing of consequence to judge.

It might be thought that the chattering mind's purpose in imposing the judgments of "good" and "bad" on the reality of our experience is to permit us to pursue whatever is pleasurable and avoid whatever is not. Despite the intuitive appeal of this theory, "pleasure" and "pain" are not so separable, except in the conviction of our chattering mind, and the operation of our egotism is actually even more devious than this theory would suggest. Judgmentalism is actually driven by our egotism's compulsion to repeat, as if by this means it could guarantee and perpetuate its own deluded "reality." The compulsion to construct judgments and then for the chattering mind to repeat them incessantly assures our egotism that it is "for real," that it is king of its dominion.

Notice how our judgments are always about the self, even when they appear directed against the other, and notice how they always bolster our egotism's sense of its existence and importance, even when they are judgments against the self. While it is in our egotism's interests to condemn the other and elevate the self, our chattering mind would sooner condemn the self and elevate the other than let go its compulsive attachment to rendering and repetitiously pronouncing its judgments. Evidently, an other-condemnatory judgment makes our egotism feel both that it really exists and that it is superior, but even a self-condemnatory judgment serves to assure our egotism that what it calls its reality really does exist. Condemning, hating and attacking the other as "bad" serves our egotism by making it feel "good" and "real." Yet self-condemnation, self-hatred and self-torture also gratify our egotism by supporting its deluded sense of mastery. Our egotism founds itself on its fearfulness of our erotic energies, and it attempts to substantiate and secure itself by means of the repetition compulsiveness of its own judgmentalism.

Judgmentalism actually occurs by a partial transmutation of the bodymind's erotic energies into the forces of malice. It is always reactive, originating in our egotism's terror of its own dissolution. Judgmentalism is intrinsically fear-based and hostile, deriving its repetitious force by co-opting or "scoring" off our sexual-spiritual energies. Thus, in the origin of our judgmental compulsivity, the energies of libido, kundalini or *prāna*, are partially transmuted into the hostile activities of separation and subjugation.

Judgmentalism is the origin of all human malice. It damages every individual. It damages the human community. It damages the entire planet. It inscribes itself throughout our bodymind, not only in repetitively compulsive patterns of thought, feeling and action, but also in somatic tension, constriction and blockage. Judgmentalism is our egotism's way of enclosing itself against the flowing power of our potential to experience the joy, ecstasy and bliss of our erotic sourcing. The ultimate terror for our egotism is that we live life in Love.

Instead of surrendering to its dissolution in the supreme flow of Love, our egotism chatters as if it could be king—dominant, invincible, and everlasting. Yet it is constantly terrified of the erotic momentum of deathfulness within—fundamentally fearful of the power of our sexual-spiritual energies to dissolve it into the ecstatic emptiness of Love, the supreme Sacred Unity of being and nonbeing. Ultimately, our egotism cannot succeed in its grandiose ambitions. Its only "success" is to burden us with shame and guilt over our erotic potential, which is the very sourcing of our enlightening. Despite its frantic accomplishments and vain strategies, our egotism cannot ultimately be king. Our chattering mind beats repetitively on the hollowness of its own compulsions. Our egotism may imprison us in its grip, keeping us deluded and unawakened, but truthfully this is ultimately a fragile, frantic, and futile agenda. It is the origin of all our disease. Yet our egotism will bloat itself again and again, until we make peace with our own irreparable insufficiency, inadequacy, and impermanence—until we release ourselves fully to the bliss of our erotic enjoyment. Yet, most often, we resist the liveliness of life; our chattering mind's attachment to judgmentalism and the egotistic force of our malice strive to suffocate the erotic exuberance of our Holy Spirit. The only response to this imprisonment is our liberation through spiritual practice.

# VI

## The Essentials of Spiritual Practice

If Holy Spirit flows all around, through and within us, then our spiritual calling is to align that which is within our bodymind with the supreme flow of the universe, which is that of the truthfulness of Love. This alignment is a process of enlightening ourselves, of unsettling the "self" or egotism of our chattering judgmental mind so as to open ourselves to the light of the divine. Spiritual life takes practice, and practice, and practice. Yet however great its challenges and its hardships, life on the spiritual path becomes ever more joyous, ecstatic, and blissful.

In these writings, we discuss the three essential "principles of method," five essential aspects, and three essential characteristics or "consequences" of life lived authentically on the spiritual path.

The threefold methodical principles of spiritual practice are entirely entwined: Spiritual practices work and play to release ourselves from our egotism, to cultivate the erotic potential of our bodymind, and do so in a way that guides us on a life's path that is ethical, existential and experiential.

In thus aligning ourselves with our Holy Spirit, we find that there are five interlinking aspects of this path:

• Spiritual practices move us behind, beside or beyond all our stories, and divest us of all our dichotomies of ideas and beliefs, of identities and positions, including all those of ideology and gender. The spiritual path is not about faith or creed, and is disinterested in dogma. For the spiritual life cannot be grasped by the constructions of our logic and rhetoric, and its processive wisdom subverts the productive judgmentalism of the chattering mind. Spiritual practice is not about refining our thoughts, feelings and actions, but about loosening our fear-based attachment to them. It is not about doing, but about being-in-the-world as the Compassionate Witness that releases us from the craving and clinging of our egotism. The way of spiritual practice is not to attach ourselves to yet another representation, but to dance in the aliveness of the presence of Holy Spirit; to dance out of our imprisonment in the edifice of our egotism; to be spiritually-in-process, without formulated destination or worries about past/ futures that do not exist; to be living fully in the here-and-now of our spiritual experience.

• Spiritual practices confront taboo, and so move us into an ethical timespace that is disinterested in rules, codes, social standards and cultural conventions. The spiritual path transgresses and transcends in a way that is entirely ethical. In our everyday life, we encounter innumerable obstructions to the free-flow of our sexual-spiritual energies. Sociocultural restrictions and regulations appear to constrain our freedom, constituting externalized constraints that bind our conduct. Blocks, tensions and constrictions within our bodymind comprise internalized constraints that inhibit the spontaneity of our erotic expression. The spiritual life invites us to detach ourselves from our fearful investment in how others judge us, to transgress sociocultural rules and codes in whatever way we are guided by Holy Spirit, to release ourselves from our own internalized inhibitions, and to transcend our society, culture and psyche by opening and expanding ourselves into our bliss. On the path of spiritual practice, Love is the only "law."

• Spiritual practices serve to liberate us from conflict, anxiety and suffering that is based on the shame, guilt, and fearfulness intrinsic to our egotism's emotional transactions. On the spiritual path, we dance naked. To release ourselves from judgmentalism is to dance out of our imprisonment in anxiety and conflict. It is almost impossible to overestimate the extent to which our unawakened minds enslave us by the force of shame and guilt. Shame is the fundamental sense that "I am not worthy," and guilt is the fundamental sense that "I am worthy of punishment." Together they constitute our most forceful resistances to allowing ourselves to come to our spiritual awakening. Our egotism manufactures these feelings, keeping them guarded in our unconscious where they exert a forceful and pernicious influence on our consciousness. Most of our shame and guilt is not apparent to our self-reflections, but inscribed by our egotism within the fibers of our bodymind, deterring us from our spiritual path, and keeping us out of the light of Love. Emancipating ourselves from shame and guilt, from anxiety and the innermost turmoil of conflict within is the challenge of our spiritual life. Spiritual practice invites us to release ourselves from the malice that our egotism has domesticated within our bodymind, as unconscious fantasy and as somatic blockages. This path invites us to transgress and transcend whatever obstructs the free-flow of the divine energies of our lifeforce.

•   Spiritual practice joyously embraces death-in-the-midst-of-life, and so fully accepts the fundamental emptiness of human existence, surrendering ourselves to the supreme ecstasy of Love. The spiritual life accepts deathfulness—the inadequacy, insufficiency, and inherent impermanence of all that our egotism constructs for us—because it permits us to understand the folly of our chattering mind's ambitions and its incessant struggle to aggrandize and immortalize itself with its repetition compulsive judgmentalism. Spiritual practice relishes the joy in the liveliness of life, embracing the integral deathfulness of this life. Our process on this spiritual path frees us from suffering, because we dance out of our imprisonment in our egotism's attachment to the outcome of life's events. Such practice liberates us from suffering by refusing our egotism's futile game of trying to avoid life's hardships, pain and loss. On this path, we find a special spiritual secret, which our chattering mind deems incomprehensible, and this is the secret of enjoying—finding the joy in—all of life's contingencies, whatever their outcome, and of facing with equanimity the vicissitudes of pleasure and pain. With this secret, the spiritual life moves us into ecstasy and bliss—for in this we surrender ourselves to the emptiness that is the energizing lifeforce of Love.

• Spiritual practice is all about celebrating the exuberant abundance of our erotic energies, mobilizing our sexual-spiritual potential into alignment with the supreme flow of the universe, which is that of the truthfulness of Love. Our miraculous universe is a vast interweaving of energies, and our lives are sparkling vibrations of Holy Spirit flowing erotically through the anatomical structures and physiological functions of our embodiment. Our bodymind is blessed, called to be a conduit for our erotic potential, which is the celebration of the divine. As libido, kundalini or *prāna*, flows exuberantly and abundantly within us, we weave and reweave ourselves into life's cosmic union. The kinesis of our erotic expression facilitates our spiritual alignment, in which we experience how heaven is here-and-now, rather than there-and-then. In our lovemaking, we have the potential to dance in the awareness that is both heaven-inspiring-to-earth and earth-aspiring-to-heaven, for this twofold timespace is One. Above all else, spiritual practice involves the enjoyment of our sensual embodiment, and celebrating the exuberance and abundance of our erotic potential, as the path of our spiritual awakening, and as the manifestation of Holy Spirit within us.

There are three hallmarks, or characteristics, of a person who is devoted to living life authentically on the spiritual path. They are written here as invitations to:

➢ Love yourself as an embodiment of Holy Spirit—more accurately, allow yourself to fall into Love, and fall out of your egotism—loving so radically that you embrace joyously the deathfulness of your being-in-the-world.

➢ Understand that all others—and all things that appear as other to you—are aspects of yourself, and embrace them in accordance with this wisdom.

➢   Live only in the present moment—for here-and-now is the presence of divine reality, the presence of the Sacred Unity of ecstatic emptiness—and dance exuberantly and abundantly your full erotic potential for joy and bliss.

There is truthfulness in this teaching, to which our egotism desperately blinds us: The spiritual path requires the practice of sexual enjoyment. Our egotism cannot tolerate the notion of our erotic freedom, for it builds its edifice precisely as an attempt to avoid being swept away by the effulgence of our erotic potential, precisely in order to avoid being dissolved into the light of Love. So our chattering mind peddles various versions of "spirituality" that eschew or repudiate our sexual-spiritual nature. There is, however, no spiritual life without the celebration of life itself, and it is the erotic potential within us that calls us to surrender to life's Sacred Unity. We are called to the path that our egotism most fears, the path that invites our erotic energies to burn our egotism in their fire.

# VII

## Celebrating our Sexualities

"The supreme God/dess delights in sexuality"—so it is written in an ancient Vedic text. In our sexuality we access the divinity that is all around us and within us. Only through our lovemaking, through the mobilization of our erotic energies, can we access a momentum powerful enough to melt the edifice of our egotism, thus aligning our humanity with the divine Sacred Unity that embraces us all. Lovemaking, which means surrendering to the Love that energizes the universe and casts our egotism into ecstatic emptiness, is the essence of spiritual practice. It is our sacred calling.

Our sexuality is ultimately mysterious, yet we know its expression to be our bodymind's connectedness with the divine, our only way of inviting Holy Spirit to fulfill our lives. Sexuality on the spiritual path involves the sensual experiencing of our embodiment. It involves finding joy in the erotic experiences of our flesh. It involves the vibration of subtle energies within and through our embodiment, a mobilizing of the sacred flow for which we may offer ourselves as a conduit. And it ethically involves our mind, both in the dissolution of the chattering mind that bolsters our egotism, and in the cultivation of spiritual awareness—the cultivation of an ethical "mindfulness" by which we surrender to the holiness of the lifeforce that vibrates around, within and through our being-in-the-world.

Our sexuality is intrinsically freeing, subverting the moralizing judgmentalism with which our egotism attempts to restrict and constrict it. If "sex" is not freeing, then it has been appropriated by the ambitions of our egotism; if it is not consensual, ethical, and freeing, it is not authentically sexual. At its sourcing, sexuality is the movement of the lifeforce within our embodiment. It links us to the mysteries within and all around us, taking us out of the entrapments of our logical and rhetorical minds. And so it offers us the supreme resource by which we may return ourselves to spiritual grace.

Our sacred sexuality is not limited to this or that mode of expression. Our bodymind is an awesomely sensitive and sensual organism, a testimony to the divine ingenuity for enjoyment. There is something profoundly miraculous about the exuberant and abundant multiplicity of our sexual responsiveness. We are blessed with the ability to find all sorts of enjoyment through our bodymind, and we are blessed with sensitive and sensual bodies that spontaneously offer us these gifts. How we cultivate this spiritual enjoyment, the process of finding the joy in our bodymind's experience, is how we worship. These sacramental acts may be expressed in manifold ways.

We are born polysexual, and sexual-spiritual practice is available to all of us, whatever the condition of our body or the state of our mind. This path is for those who are sick as much as for those who are not, for those who are handicapped as much as for those who are not, and for those who judge themselves "sinners" as much as those who would be "saints." The practice also leads us to transcend our chattering mind's dichotomies that would limit us to identifying ourselves as this or that—this or that gender, this or that orientation, this or that lifestyle. Sexual-spiritual joy is accessible to all who are alive, to anyone with any capacity for the sensuality of embodied enjoyment. It is ultimately the only viable and vital response to the anguish of our human dis-ease.

The sexual-spiritual path reengages our embodiment in relation to the outside and the inside worlds. So this practice starts with the celebration of our nakedness. Jesus of Nazareth, in the gnostic teachings of the *Nag Hammadi Library*, was clear that "God" only appears to us when we remove our clothing and our defenses, becoming naked without shame or guilt, like children in the exultant sensuality of their innocence. He was clear that, unless we return and become like children, we cannot enter the holiness of heaven-on-earth. "Returning" to our Holy Spirit means divesting ourselves of our shame, our guilt, and our fear of being who we are. And, as the Koran clearly tells us, our spiritual life means that we are all returning.

By shedding our egotism's fear, we come to face the world outside ourselves as we truly are, and in the freedom of this nakedness we also reawaken the Holy Spirit within. Sexual-spiritual practice also starts with our awareness of the movement of erotic energies inside us. According to Thomas' transcriptions, the mystical Jesus, when asked the evidence for the divine within us, responded that we know it through our pulsations of "motion and rest." As we become aware of this momentum within us, we become able to cultivate and intensify this power, to mobilize our erotic potential.

This mobilization of our sexual-spiritual potential may be engaged in many different ways. Releasing ourselves to complete nakedness, as well as surrendering ourselves to the joyous and rhythmic dancing, the spontaneous movements, of our entire bodymind, is the essence of erotic arousal, embarking us on our sexual-spiritual path. This awakening, through our erotic arousal and then through our orgasming, may be invited through any medium of our bodymind—through erotic sensitivities throughout our body and all over the tenderness of its skin surface, and through mindfulness of the deep stillness that underlies our waking consciousness.

Most of us live in conditions of touch deprivation that retard our spiritual awakening. Whatever our background, whatever the sociocultural taboos, the impulse to return to touching and being touched is a cry for the serenity that comes through accessing the divinity within. Consensual touching, whatever else it may also be, expresses our longing to reground ourselves in our capacity to experience Love, to return to the still vibrancy of the unity of Love through the erotic sensitivity and sensuality of our embodiment.

Our genitals have a unique role in this awakening, and although spiritual awareness can be initiated without the full functioning or the immediate participation of our genitals, it is a profound spiritual secret that the glories of our genitals are the altar for spiritual practice. Spiritual life can proceed without such an altar, but why would we shortchange ourselves by choosing such an option? Our genitals are uniquely powerful in facilitating our sexual-spiritual momentum—this is why our chattering mind makes them a major focus for our shame and guilt.

Our genitals are to be worshipped, not only because they are breathtakingly beautiful, but also because our pelvic floor holds for us an abundant resource of erotic energies—this is the lifeforce, or *prāna*, of the kundalini energies, which are also known as the dancing "Shakti" energies, for which the "Shiva" form of our embodiment is the container. Our pelvis houses the "root" or *mulādhāra* and the "flow" or *svādhishthana* chakras, which are the key sourcing of our erotic energies, our potential for passion and flow, as well as a major way in which the lifeforce enters our embodiment. In celebrating our sexual-spiritual path, we arouse and intensify the energies of these chakras, arousing the fire within. We pleasure our genitals with the touch of our skin, with the hands, with our mouths, with the anal orifice, with the consortion of other genitals, and by internally flexing the musculature of the pelvic floor. In so doing, we stoke the inner fire, and we may draw it upward by our breath, movement and sounding out our vibrations.

The rippling, undulating, vibrating, orgasming dance of energies through the channels of our embodiment is our path of joy, ecstasy and bliss. Its momentum burns away the hindrances, blocks, resistances and obstructions that our egotism positions in its path. Our chattering mind is stilled by the flowing intensity of the energies of the lifeforce, tracked for us by our breathing, moving, and sounding out its vibrations. Sexuality is always a dance of lovemaking, when dancing is the sexual-spiritual practice of breathing, moving, sounding, and flowing in the vibrations of our sacred energies.

As our erotic energies become more free-flowing, we become aligned with the lifeforce of the cosmos, and our subtle energies move freely from our *mulādhāra* or "root" chakra, through our *svādhishthana* or "flow" chakra, through our *manipura* or "power" chakra in the stomach, through the heart or *anāhata* chakra, through our *vishuddha* throat chakra from which we speak the truthfulness of our being-in-the-world, and through our *ājnā* or "third-eye" chakra, to our *sahasrāra* or crown.

With this free-flow, our chattering mind is silenced and our egotism dissolves. This rippling and undulating of our erotic energies aligns and unifies us, opening us to union with the divine rhythm and spiritual grace of the universe. Through the mindfulness of our breathing, our moving, and our sounding the vibrations of our embodiment, we surrender to our bliss. This is our orgasming. As we become unified, our judgmentalism fades away. In bliss we no longer separate inner and outer, and the "me" disappears, as we float into the divine. We become "at one" not only within ourselves, and with the other persons who may be our partners, but also with the trees, the skies, the mountains, and the oceans. The alienated, separated and incessantly judgmental "me" disappears into the joyous momentum of the lifeforce, which carries us into orgasmic ecstasy as our erotic energies dance freely within and through the lovemaking of our embodiment. This is the essence of all meditation. It is how we come into a meditative process, and how we access the magnificence of our Holy Spirit.

In sexual-spiritual union with our Beloved, we come to an awareness of our divinity, an awakened mindfulness that is the lifeforce itself. We no longer identify with our craving and clinging, with our possessions and our attachments; we are no longer fearful of the deathfulness of life itself. We are no longer identified with our egotism, and consequently our egotism deflates and disappears. We become the lifeforce itself; we become our *prāna*, in the very presence of which we are the Compassionate Witness that lovingly sees all things and lets them go.

And who is the "Beloved" with whom we are to achieve this sacred union? We may engage our erotic potential in the bedroom, the torture chamber, or out in the beauties of nature. We may engage it when we are infirm or when we are in peak condition.

We may engage these sexual-spiritual practices as an erotic solo, with an erotic partner of either gender, or with an erotic group. The "Goddess" delights in all manner of erotic engagements. Indeed, if we exclude anyone or anything from the embrace of our erotic potential, we fall back into the snares and delusions of our chattering mind. If our ethical intent is the dissolution of our judgmental egotism, there can be no "right" or "wrong" way to express our erotic potential. Our sexual-spiritual life is amoral—indifferent to the rules and regulations established by human judgmentalism—yet it is profoundly and inherently ethical. Our sexual-spiritual path follows the erotic enjoyment of our embodiment, and we do not try to imagine that we can control where Holy Spirit will lead us.

Who is the Beloved, with whom we are to unite in orgasmic exultation? As generations of Sufi mystics such as Jelāluddin Rumi, have shown us: It is our own divine self; it is our own divine self that we find to be the divine self of our partners and the divine self of all living entities; it is our own divine self that is the divine self of the entire universe. In the sexual-spiritual path of our own erotic unification, we come into union with the Sacred Unity that is the only One.

# VIII

## Mistaken "Spirituality"

Our egotism is clever and cunning. There is no spiritual life without sexuality, yet it is the deceit and delusion of our egotism to tell us this is not so. Remember: Our story-telling and belief-ridden mind engages in its incessant constructional activity precisely to stem the freedom of expression of our erotic energies. In the cause of this ambition, our egotism establishes for us all manner of religious and political organizations to promote the message—by persuasion and persecution—that only through curbing and censoring our erotic potential could we ever achieve our "spiritual reward."

Our egotism exploits our spiritual longings, enticing us with countless "spiritual" endeavors that actually function to deprive us of our spiritual energies. Most conspicuously, our egotism derails our spiritual longings by leading us into the fraud and violence of "organized religion." In this sense, religious orthodoxies, as much as they may express and reflect our yearning for the spiritual life, cannot disentangle themselves from their moralizing judgmentalism or from the edifice of their institutional organization. Spiritual life involves dancing our Holy Spirit—and this dancing is an ethical and existential experience that has virtually nothing to do with our subscription or subjugation to any particular system of beliefs. Our beliefs, so dear to our chattering mind, merely get in the way of our spiritual path. To be on our spiritual path, we merely have to trust in the experiential wisdom of our embodiment, the truthfulness of Holy Spirit.

Authentic spiritual life has nothing to do with narratives about the meaning of life, about the retroactive significance of the past, or the proactive promise of the future. Rather, it concerns our living experience of the liveliness of life itself, the presence of our erotic potential. Authentic spiritual life has nothing to do with professions of faith, or with mythematic stories about a nonexistent "there-and-then." It has nothing to do with moralizing strictures, ceremonial observances, psychic phenomena, supernatural occurrences or superstitious prognostications, magical incantations, the "power of positive thinking," or theological deliberations about what allegedly came "before" and what awaits us "after." All such chattering actually evaporates in the fire of authentic spiritual experience, which is always and forever our experience of Holy Spirit here-and-now.

Everything we seek spiritually is already in the here-and-now of our sexual embodiment. It is our erotic presence, flowing around, within and through ourselves. Its access requires no beliefs, no faith in stories, no compulsive ceremonies, no magical devices, no organized institutions, and no moralizing judgmentalism. Only the pervasive and perverse forcefulness of our egotism prevents us from seeing this. The portal of Holy Spirit flows all around, through and within us. We need only knock upon our own door, and allow ourselves to enter.

Religion is founded by the procrastinations of our egotism, which refuses to accept the invitation of Holy Spirit—since this would entail its own dissolution—and so insists that there must be a prerequisite faith, a profession of belief, a history of observance, or the permission of some authority. "Our ecstasy and bliss cannot be here-and-now," according to the killjoy constitution of our chattering mind, "it has to be there-and-then, and it has to be ordained by proper authority." In support of this mistake, religious and political organizations are produced.

What "authority" is needed? The most notable "authority" is generated by our belief in a personified "God" that can be formulated by our chattering mind. There are at least five consequences to this.

First, once "God" is personified, authentic spiritual practice becomes bankrupted in favor of deliberations over what our egotism might choose to believe about this "God"—and we may note here that, sooner or later, every such "God" always ends up promulgating quite stringent opinions that would censor or curb humanity's erotic freedoms.

Second, what is called "spiritual life" comes to involve an obsessive series of negotiations between "us" and "God." It becomes not only necessary that we believe, but also that we behave as "He" prescribes, and our prayerfulness becomes a matter of petitioning for "His" favors or praising "His" endowments.

Third, "God," once personified—and even when our notion of "God" is not personified, but rather a representation of some "Absolute Idea" or "Absolute Ideal" that we are not—is invariably in the business of making us feel shame and guilt about being ourselves, simply because we always fall short of this notion of perfection.

However, fourth, since this personified "God" usually favors those who believe and pray to "Him" in the proper manner, the devout may—despite their intrinsic imperfection and unworthiness—become the "chosen," the "saved," the "elect," or special in some manner. Those who are thus selected for their correct subscription, good conduct or appropriate belief are guaranteed to receive their due rewards in some timespace—that is rarely here-and-now, but usually there-and-then.

Fifth, since the "spiritual" superiority of those who are devout to this "God" is thus assured, it becomes perfectly appropriate to coax, coerce or kill those who lack faith in this particular version of "God," or who adhere to some other personified image of "Him," and to do so "in God's name." Hostility and violence to others is thus endemic to every religious faith—however much "love" may be paraded as its central preaching.

Does not all of this reek of the logic and rhetoric of our egotism? Yet such chatter pervades the theology of our religious faiths. It pertains to traditions such as the Hindu with all its derivatives, the Confucian, and the Shintō, as well as many native faiths, in which the deity may either have multiple personas, or be represented as a rather abstract sort of ideal principle or notion of perfection.

And it pertains dramatically to the "religions of the book"—Judaism, Christianity and Islam—with their many variants, for these faiths consistently tend to prioritize judgment over compassion. With these religions, the history of ingroup/outgroup fighting has done untold damage to our humanity and to the planet we inhabit. Yet in all these religions, and not just those whose orthodoxy is located in the authority of a book, "spiritual life" is routinely mistaken for the refinement of our judgmentalism.

What "authority" is needed to ordain the propriety of "religious faith"? Although the most notable authority is belief in a "God" that can be formulated by our chattering mind, three other sorts of political authority are also invariably established by our egotism's ambition to thwart our authentic spiritual experience: the authority of the "middleman," the authority of the religious institution, and the authority of egotistic "spiritual" beliefs.

Once "God" is personified, and formulated as being somewhere outside of us, our egotism is quick to recruit a "middleman" to support our relationship with "Him." And when "God" is formulated as a more abstract principle, the need for "experts" to embroider the formulation may be even more urgent. Inspirational figures and clergy of all sorts are installed to perform these functions. Saints, gurus and priests augment our interpretation of "God's will"—invariably becoming "spiritual" entrepreneurs who serve the needs of our own, and often also their own, egotism. Along with these entrepreneurial endeavors, the cultural institutions of religion are formally established—not only the social associations connected with synagogues, churches, or mosques, but also all the economic, political, legal, and military structures and organizations that legitimate themselves by their association with a particular theological system of belief.

To sustain its beliefs, our egotism needs a social community of belief, as well as an "other"—an outgroup, whose egregious failure to believe may be condemned. A hallmark of the suppression and repression of authentic spiritual experience is the extent to which religions operate by making individuals fit within, or adapt to, the prevailing sociocultural context. Those whose beliefs and conduct "fit" well are praiseworthy; those who do not are—sooner or later—pronounced contemptible. Our story-telling and belief-ridden mind is well adapted to the sociocultural circumstances that are its own expression. Religions peddle moralizing ideologies—they instruct us how to think or what to feel, and they promote the "right" way to conduct ourselves. All this is always a distraction from spiritual life; more often, it is the means by which we are blinded to our spiritual experience.

To sustain its beliefs, our egotism also needs to convince us that it has privileged rights over all manner of "spiritual" matters. If any serendipitous circumstance of "good fortune" comes to us, our chattering mind is always ready to tell us that "God," or indeed the entire universe, must be acting in our favor. Our egotism tries to recruit "spiritual" practices to its own advantage, using ceremonial observances, proclamations of psychic powers, magical recitations, and the petitioning of "prayer," to promote its own emotional comfort and material wealth. "Because we believe," our chattering mind tells us, "our superiority, over those who don't, is well proven, just look at this-and-that circumstance." And, if circumstances suggest the opposite, then our chattering mind offers another story: "Sure, our lives feel inferior now, and others seem to have better fortune, but we are special—either because we are God's chosen, or because our faithful belief in God will grant us salvation—and so we will be proved superior in the there-and-then, when we will be richly rewarded for our current troubles."

Our egotism readily subscribes to the idea that it has some special relationship with a supreme egotism by the name of "God"—a relationship that others apparently lack. Our egotism is also ready to espouse the beliefs of what is called "spiritual materialism," believing that its own petitioning of "God" can accrue us special favors; or that its own magical acts or "positive thinking" will cause the universe to bring us material rewards; or that its own activities can bring us into a special relationship with a "supreme being" or "higher power," and that this special relationship will be evident in the benefits that we receive when others do not. Along with these egotistic notions of pseudo-spiritual materialism, our egotism is very ready to imagine that there is a scale of "spiritual progress," on which people are arranged as a hierarchy ascending toward some final destination, such as "heaven" or "complete enlightenment." All these guileful beliefs are common indications of the bogus "spirituality" that our egotism invents to derail us from the authentic experience of spiritual practice. Our egotism cannot offer us the wisdom of spiritual experience, cannot afford to allow us to surrender to the divine, and is determined to distract us from our spiritual path.

Such "religious" impulses, with all their logical and rhetorical attachments, serve our egotism by drowning out the call of our sexual-spiritual experience. Matters of group affiliation, of liturgical performances, of custom and tradition, of moralizing doctrine, of theological dogma, or of bogus "spiritual" beliefs and behaviors, are all established to substitute for the exuberance and abundance of spiritual life. The theological beliefs and stories, as well as the moralizing ideologies, which comprise our religious faiths, are designed by our egotism to censor and curb our access to the spiritual exuberance and abundance that is within, here-and-now. Our egotism cannot tolerate heaven-on-earth. It perpetuates its own deluded sense of reality by incessantly representing past/futures by which to stem the flow of our erotic potential. It is no accident that the world's most prominent religions all typically propound that the "sins" of sexuality are even more grievous, and more severely punishable, than actions involving violence against life—consider orthodox Judaism, fundamentalist Christianity and Islam, as well as many of the Hindu, Confucian, Shintō, and native traditions. By one means or another, our egotism invents "God" to distract us from the godliness that is present in all that is.

All religions contain sprinklings from the fountain of spiritual insight and inspiration; but all of them promote our attachment to beliefs and stories, mistaking this attachment for spiritual practice. Authentic spiritual life spells catastrophe for our egotism, but the platitude of religious faith well suits its ambitions. Spiritual life involves the erotic dancing of Holy Spirit. The very construction of organized religion proves that we cannot both yearn for spiritual life and repudiate our sexuality. Our spiritual and our sexual longings are one, coming from one and the same sourcing.

# IX

## Mistaken "Sexuality"

Our egotism is clever and cunning. Remember: our egotism chatters fearfully in an incessant effort both to exploit the power of libidinal energy, and to control it, channelize it, obstruct it, build an edifice of beliefs and stories over it, and generally to immobilize its freedom. Our chattering mind strives to "despiritualize" and "desexualize" the power of the lifeforce within us. As if by the incessant and compulsive repetition of identities, positions, narratives, and attachments, our egotistic mind could assure itself of the validity and permanence of its own existence. Perhaps the most devious trick of our egotism occurs when it sells us the socially-approved commodity of mere "sexiness" as substitute for the power of our sexual-spiritual liberation.

To understand this, we must understand how we are all born with a magnificent polysexual potential, and how this potential is attenuated as our egotism develops itself in reaction to our successive traumatizations. As babies we may revel joyously in our sensuality, only to grow into adults who seem to have lost the exuberant playfulness of our birthright. We have discussed how our egotism develops from our fear of the deathfulness of life itself. This development is exacerbated by the traumatizations we all encounter in the course of our life, especially in our infancy and childhood. Traumatizations are those events or circumstances in which we feel that our personal experiences are misused or abused—experiences in which our sense of wellbeing is interrupted. Our traumatizations usually escalate as our egotism develops itself, as we encounter yet more situations in which the capacity of our chattering mind to believe that it is in control of life is dramatically and terrifyingly overwhelmed. Our sexuality is not only the path of our joy, ecstasy and bliss—it is also the power that portends for our egotism the deathfulness of life itself. So more and more virulently in reaction to each traumatization, our egotism becomes adversarial toward our sexual-spiritual energy. Our erotic freedom, our polysexual birthright, becomes more and more curtailed. As our socialization and acculturation proceeds, the magnificent polysexuality of our erotic potential is diminished, our sexual expression is narrowed, and we become increasingly blocked and frustrated. Our "sexuality" becomes subordinated to the imperatives of our egotism. It becomes mere "sexiness."

This is why most of us live most of our lives empty-hearted and sensually closed. We live as alienated shells of the magnificence that we are. Our chattering mind, alienated from the wisdom of our erotic bodymind, incessantly reinscribes the dissociation of our heart, our genitals, and the totality of our sensuality. As we have indicated, this is the key reason for our suffering in reaction to the liveliness of life, suffering in reaction to life's pleasures as well as its inevitable hardship, pain and loss. Our egotism tries: To have us live defended against the unavoidable experiencing of our own inadequacy and insufficiency. To have us live intolerant of the inevitability of pain and loss. To have us live terrified of our own craziness. To have us live fearful of our own death. To have us live like the "living dead," frightened of the very liveliness of life itself. To have us live refusing to surrender ourselves to the universe's supreme flow, which is that of the truthfulness of Love. And in striving to establish this agenda, our egotism systematically deprives us of our sexual-spiritual enjoyment.

However, our egotism cannot ultimately succeed. It can never be king—even with "God" on its side. It cannot succeed in averting pain and loss; it merely makes them more unbearable by having us suffer in reaction to these experiences. It can never avert the meaninglessness of life, despite all the "meanings" with which it plies us; it merely eradicates the creativity of a delightful madness, and plunges us into nightmares of utter insanity. It cannot prevent our death, despite the way in which it importunes us with fantasies of "immortal accomplishment," of "making my mark on the world," of being "remembered forever," and of life-after-death. And most blessedly, our egotism cannot ultimately expunge our erotic potential—despite the fact that it makes every effort to suppress, repress, and inhibit, the exuberance and abundance of our sexual-spiritual energies.

Because our egotism cannot ultimately expunge our sensual experience, it deviously attempts to convert our sexual-spiritual energies into the commercialized expressions of mere "sexiness"— as if to sell us "sex" and "sexiness" in order to deprive us of our erotic freedom and our path to joy, ecstasy and bliss.

Humans have often lived in the gross misery of erotic suppression, repression, and inhibition. However, because of both the homogenization of our cultural institutions and the globalization of americanized social norms, we live today in even more paradoxical and dangerous circumstances. We live in what we will call a "sexified" society in which "sex" and "sexiness" appear in every cultural medium—and in which *both* the cultural expression of these phenomena, *and* religion's official opposition toward them, serve to obstruct us from experiencing freely our sexual-spiritual enjoyment.

On the one side, we find references and allusions to sex very much on the surface of our lives in the everyday world. But it is, almost always, a commercialized exploitation of sexiness. It is "sexuality" alienated from the spiritual energies of our embodiment. What our egotism promotes and peddles is sexiness as a commodity—titillating, sensationalistic, exciting-but-banal. This is "sexuality" that has been appropriated to our egotism's ambitions, operating by disavowal or denial of its own beauty and profundity. Although there is nothing "wrong" with taking pleasure in these commodities, our spiritual awakening makes us aware of the force with which they may distract us from the authentic enjoyment of our full erotic potential.

On the other side, we find vehement adversaries of this sexiness—a viciously illiberal rightwing with escalating economic and political power, speaking in the name of religious righteousness, dogma and fundamentalism. We live in a troubled world in which fundamentalisms of all varieties are gaining adherents at an alarming rate, catapulting us toward the suicide of our species and planetary destruction. The central mandate of this adversarial stance is the persecution and elimination of those who politically assert their freedoms. This persecution is rationalized as "the need to protect" an illusory majority from such "dangers to society" as feminists, gays, those who insist on the freedom to control their own bodies, all manner of nonconformists, individuals who follow alternative lifestyles, and anyone who revels in erotic entertainment. Whether or not we realize this, what we are observing—with the burgeoning of fundamentalist dogma in all its varieties, worldwide—is, at its common core, the rise of "sexual fascism."

Both the sexification of our world and the fundamentalist antagonism towards its expression serve our egotism's anti-sexual ambitions. We know that behind, beneath and beyond this sexification, human sexuality is inherently and intrinsically spiritual in a way that is profoundly frightening to our chattering mind. Yet the phenomenon of sexification takes "sex" and exploits it toward the goals of our egotism. "Sexuality" becomes pivotal to the chattering mind's agenda of domination, hostility, coercion and violence. "Sex" becomes a mechanism for perpetuating the hindrances, resistances, obstructions and blockages to the free-flow of our sexual-spiritual energies. And it is crucially important to understand this paradox: Fundamentalist and fascist opposition to the phenomena of sexification pursues the same goal as the mechanisms of sexification itself, namely that of depriving us of our sexual-spiritual energies. This hostile and self-righteous opposition merely advocates a different mechanism—suppression, repression, and inhibition, as distinct from the compulsivity of sexification. Beneath the surface appearance of antagonism, these adversarial tendencies in the sociocultural arena are both terrified and united in their suppression and repression of our erotic potential.

Our egotism encourages our preoccupation, both with this sexification and with opposition to it, on the condition that this preoccupation reduces "sexuality" to a banal commodity of social communication and exchange, rather than allowing us to experience the vibrant and powerful spiritual energy that sexuality authentically is. Our egotism tries to force us to reduce "sexuality" to the commodity of sexiness, to matters of gender politics, to the mechanics of reproduction, or to a narrow and fragmented litany of routinized behaviors called "sex." Despite the profusion of "sexual" images on the surface of everyday life in today's world, we continue to be as terrified as ever of the deeper expression of our sexual-spiritual energies. Our egotism is frightened of our access to the divine.

Our sexual-spiritual being-in-the-world subverts and subverses our egotism's intrinsic commitment to domination, hostility, self-righteousness, coercion and violence. Our erotic sourcing naturally follows what psychoanalysis has called the "law of laws"—it naturally respects the boundaries of incestuous contact—and it naturally expresses the transcendent law of Love. What this means, most profoundly, is that if our conduct is not consensual, ethical, flowing and free, it is not truly sexual. Rather, it is our egotism's deceit, the trickery of "sexification," by which our chattering mind tells us that we are "doing sex" when in reality we are avoiding the calling of our erotic potential.

Authentic sexuality is consensual and embraces the entire universe of every interconnected being-in-the-world. It is inherently ethical, flowing and free. It is the exuberant and abundant expression of the liveliness of life itself. Authentic sexuality is always spiritually awesome, for our sexuality is our access to Holy Spirit, to the godliness that pervades all things. Sexuality is our spirituality in motion.

# X

## Tantra as Ethicality (without Moralizing)

We move on our sexual-spiritual path as soon as we give up our ideas about a personified "God" that our chattering mind can formulate, and as soon as we relinquish our notions of some "Absolute Ideal" or state of "Complete Perfection" by which our egotism can continue to promulgate its judgmentalism. As we let go these representations, we move ourselves into godliness, and we experience the godliness in everything, every situation, every person, and every living thing.

In this way, our sexual-spiritual energies are inherently ethical, flowing into the supreme vibration of the universe, which is that of the truthfulness of Love. This path is naturally ethical, existential and experiential. It is, however, also transgressive and transcending. Freeing ourselves from the shame, the guilt, the anxiety and the conflict, with which our lives are encumbered, requires that we break our attachment to the customary routines of "law and order." The sexual-spiritual path calls us to decondition ourselves, to unlearn the protocols of our socialization and acculturation, and to free ourselves from the imprisonment of our conditioning. Spiritual practice deconstructs all the rules, restrictions and regulations that our egotism formulates, and entails a breaking of erotic taboos, or societal standards and cultural conventions. On the spiritual-sexual path we emancipate ourselves from the moralizing ideologies so dear to our chattering mind. Our egotism thrives on moralizing ideologies, as it vindicates its existence both through self-righteousness and through self-condemnation.

Moralities close us down; ethicality opens us to the divine. Our egotism is deeply threatened by our surrendering to the ethical flow of the lifeforce itself.

Our awareness or mindfulness of ethicality brings us into alignment with the universe as we compassionately witness ourselves, opening our being-in-the-world to whatever *is*. Releasing ourselves from judgmentalism, spiritual practice opens us to whatever arises in the course of our experience. This open awareness is expansive and stretching, and it comprises an ethicality that cultivates compassion, appreciation and grace. This ethicality lives the only spiritual law, which is the law of Love. It exemplifies the effulgence of Love's vibration pulsating through the universe, and it exemplifies how aligning ourselves with this "law" breaks us out of the repetitive compulsions of our judgmentalism, frees us from our repetitive suppressions, repressions and inhibitions, dissolves our malice, and remobilizes the enjoyment of our being-in-the-world.

In the fifth century b.c.e., Gautama Buddha offered us, with insightful brilliance, some pointers for falling into Love's vibration. Usually spiritual teachers discuss these five "pointers" or precepts in the negative—as five sets of behaviors from which we should abstain or refrain. As such, they can be made to seem like just another moral code or series of "should-not" commandments. But this appearance is a mistake. This is not another moralizing ideology for our egotism to debate about, and struggle with; rather, it is a human characterization of the ethical flow of the lifeforce itself. We will consider them here-and-now as "five beautiful intentions" that subvert our egotism's ambitions. These are five modes of being-in-openness and of surrendering ourselves to Holy Spirit.

➢ *Revere Life:* Being reverential and respectful of the life of all living creatures—plants, animals and people, as well as the planet on which we live—so that, when we destroy life for our own needs, we strive to do so minimally, mindfully, and with reverential appreciation for the life we have destroyed.

➢ *Respect Belongingness:* Being respectful of what belongs with what, and what belongs to others, and minimizing any sense of our possessiveness, so as to live as simply and sanely as is feasible in our circumstances—mindful that all things are interdependent, taking into our lives only what truly belongs with us, and knowing that "belonging" is radically different from "possessing."

➤ *Celebrate the Sanctity of our Passion:* Being empathically celebratory of all the passions that humans experience, and engaging our potential for sensual pleasure joyously and ecstatically—rather than sliding into following the chattering mind's readiness to exploit passions and desecrate our sensuality.

➤ *Express our Truthfulness:* Being expressively committed to speaking, writing, and performing our truthfulness whenever and wherever we experience it, and thus honoring the godliness in all of us—rather than subscribing to our egotism's readiness to concoct deceitful strategies, to deploy manipulative tactics, and to bolster itself by bartering in the marketplace of gossip and meaningless exchanges.

➤ *Honor the Temple of our Bodymind:* Being worshipfully honoring of our own embodiment, being a worthy caretaker of its miracles, and a dedicated steward to its needs for health and healing—by providing it with the physical, emotional and intellectual nourishment that it needs, and exercising its functions in ways that enhance our spiritual wellbeing.

We can readily see that these "five beautiful intentions" are really ways of committing ourselves mindfully to ethical attitudes of openness to all that *is* and to alignment with all that *is*—which means all that is "otherwise" than that which our egotism reinforces. Such intentions or spiritually-grounded "attitudes" create an ethical timespace that is the opening for Love's vibration. This is radically distinct from the strictures of moral codes, societal standards, and cultural conventions, to which our egotism is doggedly attached.

When we allow the ethicality of our erotic potential—rather than attaching to our egotism's struggles with "sexual morality"— the radical distinction becomes dramatically clear. To talk of "sexual morality" is to mistake the authentic nature of our erotic potential. It is to chatter incessantly about who should not touch what, who should not pleasure whom, and so forth. The anti-sexual and anti-spiritual implications of such chatter are never far from the surface, and its tone of judgmental condemnation, fostering inhibition, prohibition, and addiction, is always apparent. Moralizing ideologies function to block our erotic potential. In the "success" of their observance, they support our egotism by promoting suppression and repression; in the "failure" of their observance, they support our egotism by promoting compulsivity and "sexification." Authentic spiritual practice celebrates our erotic potential, ethically and amorally. On the sexual-spiritual path, the mandates of our society and culture become a matter of pure irrelevance. The sexual-spiritual path frees us from shame and guilt about ourselves and our erotic energies. Insisting that we fall off this path, our egotism plunges us back into the imprisonment of shame, guilt, anxiety and conflict. Once we embark on the tantric path—devoting ourselves to accessing, weaving and reweaving our sacred energies—we are called to let go of, to release ourselves from, everything our egotism holds dear.

# XI

## Tantra as Method (without Technique)

There are no techniques for sexual-spiritual practice; there are no decisions to be made; there are no strategies, rules, or goals to be determined; there are neither instructors nor an instruction manual; and there are no preliminaries. Techniques, decisions, strategies, rules, goals, expectations, destinations, and measures of outcome, are the trademark of our egotism. They are the instruments employed whenever our chattering mind determines that something must be changed, and they imply a forced approach to growth that keeps our egotism very much in charge. So there are no specific instructions, and ultimately no external authorities, on the sexual-spiritual path, because the way in which each person proceeds on this path is profoundly individual. Only from the wisdom of our own embodiment, only by accessing our Holy Spirit, can we heal ourselves. And we can only do so by embracing our erotic potential here-and-now. This is why Taoists, since Lao-Tzu's writing around the fifth century b.c.e., have considered this the "pathless path."

There are, however, three "principles of method" for our sexual-spiritual life:

➢ We practice by working and playing to release ourselves from the imprisonment of our egotism. This requires the challenges of unlearning, deconditioning, deconstructing and transgressing so as to loosen our attachment to our judgmentalism, to still our chattering mind, and thus dissolve the fear-based edifice of our egotism. The tantric secret of this is meditation, in which we become a Compassionate Witness that lovingly sees all the productions of our egotism, but does not identify with them, and thus lets them go by.

➤ We practice by cultivating the erotic potential of our embodiment. This requires that we relax into our passionate and profound enjoyment of the lifeforce within us, inviting the free-flow of our sexual-spiritual energies and thus aligning our genitals, our heart, and our entire bodymind with the supreme flow of the universe. The secret of this is again the meditative or tantric "attitude," which frees our enjoyment of our erotic energies from their obstruction by our egotism, and through which we find that our Compassionate Witness is itself the liveliness of life flowing through us.

➤ We practice by inviting ourselves into the adventure of a life's path that is ethical, existential and experiential. As we surrender to the erotic energies of our Holy Spirit and our egotistic attachments dissolve, we become vibrantly aware of the lifeforce that is all around us and that runs within and through us. It becomes natural—conscious choice is not even needed—to revere life, to respect belongingness, to celebrate the sanctity of passions, to express truthfulness, and to honor the temple of our bodymind. The secret of this is the tantric process of enjoying our relatedness, without being attached to the outcome of our relationships; of enjoying being holiness-becoming-manifest, rather than attaching to outcomes in the business and busyness of our doing; and of enjoying, and embracing, the erotic deathfulness of life itself. We come to live in meditation—we come to live a tantric life.

Our deepest sexual desires and our profound spiritual longings call us to pursue these three principles of method. As we step onto this path, we may speak our truthfulness, articulating our intentions to move toward our enlightening, and we may hold our intention to relieve the suffering of ourselves and of others, our intention for the universe of all beings to become happy and free. This is perfectly natural. However, it is beneficial to be aware, and wary, of our egotism's urgency to appropriate these intentions for its own ambitions, recruiting our sexual desires and spiritual longings and attempting to turn them into plans and productions of its own design, requiring techniques to achieve their designated outcome. Talk of techniques and anticipated destinations or outcomes is the trademark of the ambitions of our chattering mind. We have to be awake to the many tricks with which our egotism will try to allure us and derail us from the tantric path—to deter us from our sexual-spiritual union with the Sacred Unity that is Love.

# XII

## Pointers for Sexual-Spiritual Practice

Although no teaching about this path can substitute for our immediate experience in its practice, there is a role for tantric facilitators, who are neither priests nor professors, but individuals who can share some "pointers" derived from the practices of their own enlightening. Drawing upon the wisdom of many tantric facilitators, here are thirteen interrelated pointers. They are all different ways of expressing the same three principles of method. May they be helpful for our mindfulness as we dance into our spiritual practice.

• *Remember that we are all addicts:* Our egotism is addicted to itself, addicted to the promulgation and compulsive repetitiousness of its own judgmentalism. We may also be addicted to substances, to power, to material gains, to "spiritual" chicanery, to moral superiority, or to the thrills of sexification. But our egotism is always addicted to its own ambitions and attachments—to its craving and clinging, to its insistence that it possesses reality, and to its identification with the productivity of thought, feeling, and action. For all of us, our sexual-spiritual path is a matter of stopping the practice of these addictions.

• *Cultivate our Compassionate Witness:* The unique key to letting go our addiction to judgmentalism is to cultivate the Compassionate Witness within ourselves, and devote ourselves to it as our Beloved. As we fall into the meditative attitude of awareness, we allow ourselves to become this Compassionate Witness that experiences and sees all our thoughts and feelings, as each one arises, but does not attach us to them, does not identify with them, and does not struggle to oppose or transform them. Rather, it witnesses them compassionately, appreciates them and graciously lets them go on by. In this process, our egotism ceases to score off the energies of our embodiment, and its force gradually crumbles. We discover that our Compassionate Witness is *prāna* itself, and our entire bodymind becomes open to a renewed enjoyment of our erotic potential. Cultivating this Compassionate Witness is the only way to empower our sexual-spiritual growth, and is the key to tantric practice as the unblocking, weaving or reweaving of our sacred energies.

• *Breathe into our Compassionate Witness:* The preeminent way to fall into this meditative attitude of awareness is to invite our mind's focus to rest gently on Holy Spirit within us. We can do this at each and every moment of our daily lives. Instead of investing in all the business and busyness of our chattering mind, we invite ourselves to focus on the subtle movement of the lifeforce within. This is immediately manifest to us through the flow of our breathing. It also becomes manifest as the vibrations that sound themselves all around, within and through our being-in-the-world. This is tantric meditation, and almost all of our everyday activities may be invited into it. To pursue this practice deliberately in a special timespace of our lives, we may sit in meditation. This means we sit quietly and comfortably upright, closing our eyes and ears, and we invite our focus to rest gently on the most subtle feature of our inbreath and our outbreath; then we watch when our chattering mind protests strenuously by persistently trying to distract us with impulses or fantasies, and compassionately, moment-by-moment, we thank it goodbye. This stills the chattering mind, divesting our egotism of its grip on us, and it brings us into awareness or mindfulness of the energies of our lifeforce. From a special period of daily meditation, we may extend our engagement with this meditative process throughout our everyday lives.

• *Dance, move and vibrate into our Compassionate Witness:* It is also especially powerful to meditate while dancing wildly and spontaneously, while sounding out the vibrations of our embodiment, and shaking up our chakras, arousing them passionately and whole-heartedly. Moving our bodymind energetically calms the chattering mind, and engages our erotic potential. This is an important aspect of Osho's wonderful contributions to our understanding of meditative practices, his so-called "active" or "dynamic" approaches to meditation. As we breathe, move ecstatically, sound out our vibrations, and surrender into the flow of our erotic energies, we engage our bodymind's sensuality fully, yet we are also mindful of its momentum. The wild momentum of our energies subverts the dominance of our egotism, and our Compassionate Witness is cultivated. We become, so to speak, fully "in" our body's wisdom, yet we are not entirely "of" our bodymind. Our sourcing, our lifeforce, is discovered as our Compassionate Witness. As we surrender into our wildness, we awaken into the awareness of a profound stillness within ourselves. We come to embrace the erotic deathfulness that is the liveliness of the lifeforce—the rest and motion of Holy Spirit that is our ecstatic emptiness.

• *Express our passions mindfully:* The quieting of our chattering mind does not imply a deadening of our passions, but their intensification. Our egotism, purporting to protect us from the pain and loss of life, actually deadens our experience of empathy as well as of our emotions—and, of course, ultimately this fails to protect us from anything, except temporarily from our egotism's sense of its own vulnerability. Typically, the emotionality expressed by our chattering mind is somewhat inauthentic, founded in the anxieties of our egotism, dislocated from its bodily conditions. Usually, it is either masked or paraded exaggeratively. As the fearfulness and the force of our egotism recede, and as our meditative awareness is cultivated, intense feelings arise—feelings long forgotten, inhibited, suppressed or repressed, inscribed within the connective tissues of our embodiment. In this spiritual practice, neither pain nor pleasure is to be avoided, but welcomed as expressions of the liveliness of life itself. We become as welcoming of tears as of laughter, for both express the joy of our aliveness. The genuineness of our tears washes us emotionally clean, and celebrates our empathic connectedness with all of life's pain and loss. On our spiritual path, we invite such tears to flow freely as we engage fully with the bitterness of life's experiences, as shared by all humanity. The genuineness of our laughter warms us emotionally, as our Compassionate Witness sees our folly in the face of life's pain and loss. On our spiritual path, we invite the eruptive bursts of laughter that afford us a glimpse of the ecstatic emptiness that pervades all that *is*—as if glimpsed through a crack in our egotism's deluded systems of belief. So we invite laughter to burst forth riotously as we engage fully with the sweetness of life, relinquishing our identifications and our attachments to our human deludedness. And as we invite ourselves into the fullness and the authenticity of these emotional expressions, we become aware that we are "in" them but not entirely "of" them. Our empathy and our emotionality become more mindful, as the cultivation of our Compassionate Witness frees us to celebrate the sanctity of our passions.

•   *Lovemake openly, extravagantly and expansively:* Our spiritual enlightening requires our erotic freedom. And anyway, why would we ever limit our lovemaking? Our sexuality is, after all, the process of aligning our erotic energies, and it is profoundly beneficial to all those touched by its momentum. However, it is profoundly threatening to the security of our egotism. Our chattering mind is content to have us "screw around" for, in such activities, "sexuality" is recruited to our egotism's anxiety-based program of conquest and domination. Other than the hostile possessiveness of "getting off" and "screwing around," the moralizing ideologies of our chattering mind permit us to share ourselves sensually only in closeted circumstances and only with those whom we supposedly "love." This is because genuinely erotic expression is frightening for

our egotism, which turns sexuality into an occasion for shame
and guilt. Instead, our egotism offers us compulsive sexification
in pursuit of its agenda of hostile control over the "other." Even
"at its best," our egotism's schemes of "love" are the prison-
house of attachment and possessive relationship. Genuinely
erotic freedom is the downfall of our egotism. For the relief of
our suffering, for the relief of the suffering of the human
community, and for the relief of the suffering of the planet, it
is beneficial that we engage our potential for lovemaking as
often as we are able, as fully as we are able, as passionately as
we are able, and as whole-heartedly as we are able.

   • *Lovemake exuberantly and abundantly:* At each and every
moment of our lives, our sexual expression is a blessing that we
need to free from the conditions and constraints of our egotism.
How we lovemake—whether by the gaze of our eyes, the caress
of our voice, or the gentleness of tender touching, whether with
kissing mouths and genitals, whether with or without the
consortion of vulva-vaginas and penises, whether with anal
stimulation or without—is irrelevant. What matters deeply is
the spiritual momentum of these activities. Lovemaking—
whether alone, with a stranger, with a partner we believe we
know well, with a group, or with the trees, the skies, the
mountains and the oceans—is always consensual, mutual,
wholly present, ethical, and expressive of our one heart. Such
tantric lovemaking, imbued with compassion, appreciation and
grace—as well as the heating power of passion and the cooling
power of solace in our aloneness—releases us from our chattering
mind by intensifying and circulating the erotic energies that
flow all around, within and through us. Because of this, even
the slightest engagement in lovemaking contributes to the
wellbeing of the entire universe. Lovemaking is what saves us
from our egotism. Lovemaking is the essential sacred act of
meditation. The awareness of free-flowing lovemaking is the
essence of prayerfulness.

   • *Mobilize our erotic potential into orgasming:* In the tantric
practice of lovemaking—whether this is practiced solo or with

partners—we invite our focus to rest intently and intensively on the sensual immediacy of our experience in every present moment. Our lovemaking becomes aware or mindful. It awakens and mobilizes the lifeforce within us. It becomes meditative and essentially prayerful. For example, if mouth and genital are playfully engaged, we invite our focus to rest completely and fully on the presence of these delicious sensations that we are experiencing. And as we become this sensuality, we compassionately witness any distracting thoughts or feelings that arise, understanding that these are our egotism's efforts to distract us, to recapture our energies, and to convert sexuality into its own agenda, and we mindfully thank these distractions goodbye. Such tantric lovemaking is not just a physical engagement, it becomes a meditation that circulates our erotic energies and empowers the mindfulness of our Compassionate Witness. It is a spontaneous, free and playful engagement in which we surrender ourselves to the power of the lifeforce within, and let the productions of our chattering mind pass on by. Lovemaking quietens the chattering mind, and facilitates the mobilization of erotic energies throughout our embodiment. As our energies are mobilized, we may stoke their fire and, by coordinating our breathing, our moving, and our sounding out the vibrationality within, draw them through our "inner flute" or *sushumnā*—our bodily container along the axis of the spinal column. We may stoke this fountain of fire until energies ripple and undulate from our root to our crown, exploding us into the ecstasy of orgasming. Even minor orgasmic rippling through any area of the bodymind has beneficial affects, melting our separateness and aligning us with the energies around us. But the kundalini fountain of fire that may burst up and down the sushumnā is supremely powerful in its dissolution of our egotism. This momentum is the essence of mystical experience available to us all. Such orgasming casts us into experiencing the erotic deathfulness of our existence. It joyously carries us into the ecstatic emptiness of our bliss. It opens our being-in-the-world to the inherence of heaven-on-earth. It is our union with the Sacred Unity of the supreme flow of the universe, which is that of the truthfulness of Love.

•  *Become mindful of our chattering mind:* These sexual-spiritual practices are intolerable to our egotism, which will instigate any number of hindrances, resistances, obstructions and blockages to keep us from this path. The more we approach spiritual awareness, the more we invite our Compassionate Witness into our lives, the more we awaken our erotic energies, the more threatened our egotism will be and the more reasons it will concoct to deter us from our enlightening. Our enlightening is rarely a singular epiphany that forever after insulates us from the lures and blandishments of our frightened egotism. Rather, our serenity usually comes gradually as our practice deepens and takes hold of us more fully. Our chattering mind may persist in its assertions and distractions. It will preoccupy us with narratives of past and future that take us away from the presentness of our experience. It will insist that we need to subscribe to belief systems and moralizing ideologies that prevent us from the naturalness of our ethical path. And it will generally try to convince us that we cannot survive without an edifice of identifications, positions and stories. But we can survive, and thrive. We can live life in Love. We can become the manifestation of holiness-in-process, as compassion, appreciation and grace flow freely throughout our existence and our experience. We can become orgasmically filled with joy, ecstasy and bliss. It is our egotism that cannot survive this process of being holiness-becoming-manifest. In this process, it is helpful to be aware that doing combat with our egotism actually derails us from our sexual-spiritual path. Our chattering mind actually enhances itself by the hostilities of struggle, and revels in judgmental deliberation. So to struggle against it—to argue with it, to praise it or to condemn it—is to enhance its control over us. Our egotism bloats itself as soon as we attempt to fight its influence. Opposition to our egotism is itself an act of egotism. So instead, our sexual-spiritual practice cultivates our Compassionate Witness and nurtures our erotic potential.

And, by being invited to pass on by—without any fight—by failing to gain our attachment or identification with its productions, by being thanked goodbye, our egotism gradually withers. On this sexual-spiritual path, we mindfully practice—and practice—and practice, because our egotism is usually struggling sneakily to reestablish itself.

· *Become warily aware of our egotism's allure:* Our egotism is extraordinarily tricky and deceitful, luring us back into our imprisonment and perpetuating our misery in the name of its impossible pursuit of a life without hardship, pain and loss—a life without decay and death. It is beneficial to be mindful of this. For example, our chattering mind will tell us that the "point" of life is to master the world, by which it means forcefully to dominate the other—to be a success by "achieving our potential," to gain influence and accumulate wealth. It will tell us that the "point" is to gain dominion over ourselves, by which it means our egotism's dominion over us. It will tell us that the "point" is to refine our judgmentalism, to parade our knowledge, or to preen our moralizing ideologies and religious observances. It will tell us that the "point" is not to release ourselves from belief systems, but to formulate "better" beliefs. It will tell us that the "point" is to "think positively," even though this attaches us even more tightly to the productions of our chattering. It will tell us that the "point" is to improve the transactional effectiveness of our relationships, or even to be able to "love better," by which it means to possess and control the other more effectively. And perhaps the sneakiest snares our chattering mind sets for us are that it will tell us it "knows" what spirituality is, all the while distracting us from experiencing our Holy Spirit; and that it sells us the cheap thrills of sexification, all the while deterring us from experiencing our sacred erotic potential. We need to be mindful of these entrapments. Spiritual experience is not to be found in the judgmentalism of beliefs, in moralizing conduct, in articles of faith and impressive ceremonies, in superstitious divinations, or in magical mumbo jumbo. Remember: spiritual life releases

us from the chattering mind, casting us immediately into the
erotic experience of our Holy Spirit within. Sexual experience
is ultimately not to be found in the commodities of sexification,
which either reinscribe shame, guilt, and anxiety over our erotic
potential by parading our egotism's production of sexiness, or
suborn sexual expression to our egotism's agenda of hostility
and domination. Remember: sexuality is always free-flowing,
always mutual, always an aligning of energies within the
universe touched by it, and always an opening of ourselves to
Holy Spirit that circulates all around us, within us and through
us. On our sexual-spiritual path, it is well to be mindful of
how our egotism will insist that it knows the way, and will by
this means defeat us from its own demolition.

•  *Go Wild:* The sexual-spiritual path liberates us from the
preoccupations of our egotism and from the conditioning of
our sociocultural circumstances. Celebrate our Holy Spirit! Go
wild! Celebrate life reverently! Be naked. Move into the
spontaneous dancing of our embodiment. Touch everything
and everyone with generous abandon. Sink into the eyes of the
other. Connect at the heart. Worship the genitals, for they are
altars for spiritual practice. Honor the relatedness of all things
while refusing the lure of relationships. Respect the
belongingness of things, while avoiding all possessiveness. Be
passionate, experiencing pleasure and pain as opportunities for
the enjoyment of life itself. Appreciate the sanctity of our
passions. Speak truthfulness without hesitation, and without
fear of the forces of deludedness. Nurture the temple of the
bodymind. Become yogic, understanding that yoga derives from
tantric practice. Gently unsettle all egotism and let it pass.
Cultivate the Compassionate Witness and invite our erotic
energies to flow freely. Embrace the deathfulness of the ecstatic
emptiness that pervades all being and nonbeing, understanding
that this is the universal energy of Love. Releasing ourselves to
our Holy Spirit, releasing ourselves from all our shame, guilt,
anxiety and conflict, emancipating ourselves from the
burdensome preoccupation with past and future, and

emancipating ourselves from the judgmentalism of beliefs and ideologies—freeing ourselves on this sexual-spiritual path may well cause reactions against us, for we live in sociocultural circumstances where the free are often persecuted, jailed, tortured and killed. We can, however, always access our joy, ecstasy, and bliss.

• *Celebrate the ethicality of our existence:* As we move ourselves onto the sexual-spiritual path, we release ourselves from the shame and guilt of moralizing judgmentalism, and we find ourselves naturally following the ethicality of our erotic energies. Rather than living in the edifice of our egotism with its commitment to suffering, we find ourselves living happily in compassion, appreciation and grace. As we release ourselves from our chattering mind with its incessant judgmentalism— by which it deludes us into believing that life's hardship, pain and loss, can be, and is to be, avoided—we embrace the deathfulness of life itself. In this embrace, we experience our existence fully, finding our erotic enjoyment in the liveliness of life itself.

• *Live life as a sexual-spiritual adventure:* On the tantric path, we practice, and practice, and practice. We practice living. We practice letting go our deludedness, coming into the reality of life's magnificence. Here-and-now in every present moment, we experience the divinity of existence. We find that heaven and earth are one and the same. Sexual-spiritual practice is adventure—the most adventurous adventure that humans can ever know. It requires that we constantly take ourselves "to our edge." This edge is that timespace to push further than which is to force change—which is just what our chattering mind wants, since any forcefulness validates our egotism. Yet it is also that timespace from which to hang back is to avoid growth— which is just what our chattering mind wants, since any avoidance upholds the egotism's sense of security. This is the "middle way" of which Gautama Buddha spoke, for it declines all the extremes by which our egotism becomes yet more fearful and yet more resistant to its own dissolution. Living "at our edge" is an adventure that takes us into aliveness, into an experience of the full vibrancy of existence. This sexual-spiritual adventure takes us into the timespace of the deepest innermost silence, the eternal emptiness that is the supreme flow of the universe, the truthfulness of the Sacred Unity that is Love.

# XIII

## Dancing on the *BodyPrayerPath*

The sacred spirituality that is embodied within us *is* the momentum of our sexual energies. It is *prāna* itself. Our erotic potential is Holy Spirit. These energies are the very sourcing that can most profoundly heal our fears of living joyfully in Love. And living joyfully means living life, dancing through life, in the spiritual momentum of enjoyment—of finding the joy in—of accessing compassion, appreciation and grace, even in the midst of life's inevitable experiences of emptiness, hardship, pain, loss, madness and death. At its sourcing, sexuality is the dancing movement of our lifeforce. It mobilizes and links us irrevocably to the mysteries within and around us. It takes us out of the chattering entrapments of our logical and rhetorical mind, and so offers us the supreme resource by which we may return ourselves to spiritual grace. Our egotism will not dissolve itself, and it is not ultimately concerned with our health and healing; it is only invested in its persistent ambitions. Our chattering mind cannot bring itself into alignment with compassion, appreciation and grace; it is only interested in deliberating over such matters, incessantly pronouncing judgments about what these words mean, and who is or is not endowed with these qualities. Only the wisdom of our embodiment can help us to health and healing, for the potential of our embodiment is the conduit of Holy Spirit. Sexual freedom is the way, and erotic health and healing are our spiritual practice. This is the only path to our enlightening.

As we cultivate our Compassionate Witness, we awaken ourselves and come into spiritual awareness. This awareness like fire burns away the judgmentalism of our chattering mind; just as water washes away our egotism; just as the winds of the air allow us to breathe life anew; and just as the earth returns us to the sourcing of all our sacred energies. This awareness dances us into the liveliness of life itself.

To dance the liveliness of life itself is to embrace fully and fearlessly the deathfulness that is inherent and integral to the process of life itself—the ecstatic emptiness that pervades all that is. On the spiritual path, we no longer imagine that we might be king; rather we embrace with joy our inadequacy, our powerlessness, and our imperfection. The deathfulness that is inherent and integral to the liveliness of life itself cannot be averted or overcome—embracing it is the only path of our enlightening. This is the deathfulness in the heart of us all: the deathfulness into which the dance of our orgasming casts us mysteriously, the deathfulness that we face in every authentic moment of meditation, the deathfulness that must be embraced if we are to enjoy life fully. To resist the deathfulness of life itself is to withhold ourselves from the spiritual path, it is to live life in fear, to live life by the mandates of our deluded egotism, to live life as one of the "living dead."

To live on the sexual-spiritual path is to dance our way through life's course, embracing our deathfulness at every moment of this here-and-now. The *BodyPrayerPath* is just a name given to all the many and varied tantric practices that are aspects of this way of dancing the liveliness of life. The *BodyPrayerPath* is the sexual-spiritual process of life's dancing, the dance of the Compassionate Witness, the dance of the lifeforce, the *prāna* of our erotic energies. Dancing is the breathing, moving, sounding-out the vibrations of our existence, lovemaking and orgasming our way to joy, ecstasy and bliss. This is prayerfulness. It is not "prayer," conceived by our chattering mind as an act of recitation that praises or petitions to an "other," such as "God." Rather, we must rid ourselves of the "God" of our egotism, so as to renew our connectedness with the godliness that *is* in all things. This connectedness is the prayerfulness of our embodiment: to dance is prayerful, to breathe mindfully is prayerful, to sound-out the vibrations of our experiential existences is prayerful, to lovemake is prayerful, and to orgasm into joy, ecstasy and bliss is prayerful. Prayerfulness is an aligning of the lifeforce of our embodiment with the Sacred Unity of the universe. It is the sensual process by which our human egotism is transmuted into the reality of our divine self. Prayerfulness is the dissipation of our egotism that ecstatically empties us into the existential experiencing of heaven-here-and-now-on-earth. It involves the fullness of our erotic embodiment. Prayerfulness is our dancing into the supreme flow of this universe, which is that of the truthfulness of Love.

Our egotism cannot allow our prayerfulness. Instead of dancing in this celebration, our chattering mind just chatters. It is ignorant of the dance, frightened by the reality of Sacred Unity and profoundly threatened by the intimations of life's dancing. Dancing dissolves our egotism and aligns our genitals, our hearts, and our entire bodymind with Holy Spirit.

In our prayerful dancing the here-and-now of the present, we access the deepest stillness of all that is. We access the present timespace of the "here" that absents itself, like the infinite spacelessness of points in space. We access the present timespace of the "now" that absents itself, like the infinite timelessness of moments in time. We surrender ourselves to this emptiness of real presence. This is an ecstatic emptiness that takes us out of the edifices of our egotism, and allows them to crumble, that allows all the delusional constructions, the representations of the past and the future, and all matters of egotistic importance, to dissolve away. This is an ecstatic emptiness that is the godliness within us, the Holy Spirit that brings us into compassion, appreciation, and grace, and that grants us our profound serenity.

The ecstatic emptiness of real presence is the interconnectedness of all things. It is the One: the Sacred Unity that is Love, *la-ilaha-illá'lláh*, "there is no other but God," the supreme flow that unites all being and nonbeing; the "nameless name," *Yahweh*, that cannot be spoken, cannot be formulated by our conceptual mind, cannot be put into words; the cosmic union of Shiva-Shakti; the Sacred Unity that brings together and is behind, beneath and beyond all that appears to begin and to end.

All this is in our hearts. So our sexual-spiritual practice is to align ourselves with the dancing of life's energies, the dancing of the Sacred Unity of all that *is* Love. Dancing in this way contributes to the happiness and freedom of all beings. Despite all that we are told in the snares and delusions of human egotism, there is no other way to relieve our suffering. Only dancing our lives on this *BodyPrayerPath* offers happiness and freedom for all. It is as Osho says:

*Life is celebration!*
*Celebrate life in all its forms.*
*Let the river flow in you,*
*Trust in life.*
*Accept yourself as you are and the river will reach the ocean of its own accord.*

# APPENDIX

## "Living in Meditation"

Human malice arises whenever our erotic energies are obstructed. It arises whenever we fall out of the vibration of Love. Living in meditation is the only solution to this problem.

Malice is a distinctively human propensity. It is endemic to our mind's judgmentalism, which is both the cause and consequence of obstructions and constrictions in the flow of our sensual or erotic energies—miraculous energies that infuse everything that is and is not. Malice is our propensity to hate whatever is "other" than our egotistical selves, to dwell "in our heads," and to live in conditions either of benumbed alienation, or of physical and emotional violence. It inheres to our chattering mind, which governs our lives by stories of judgment and condemnation. Malice keeps us from realizing our potential for joy, bliss and ecstasy throughout our lives.

The blessing of meditation is ultimately the only real solution to the problem of human malice, for it is the only solution that goes to the heart of the problem. It is the unique solution that addresses the problem of malice through the energies of both our heart and our sexual embodiment, rather than through the deliberations of our "head"—our judgmentally chattering mind. All other "solutions" are aimed at helping humans to improve their judgmentalism in order to make less malicious judgments and decisions in the conduct of their lives. As such, they miss the heart of the matter and perpetuate the prevalent conditions in which we are alienated from our own sexual-spiritual being.

This is because judgmentalism—this incessant productivity of our chattering mind—is the instrument of our egotism and, whatever its apparently benign or altruistic applications, judgmentalism always takes us out of the sacred vibration of Love. Despite its deceptively altruistic applications, judgmentalism inevitably ensures the malice that creates human misery and suffering. This is because, sooner or later, these apparently benign applications always show themselves to be a ploy by which our egotism is perpetuated.

The chattering judgmentalism of our egotism separates the world into categories and then decides what will be upheld and what will be repudiated. We incessantly divide the world into binary categories—such as either/or, present/absent, good/bad, pleasure/pain, life/death, me/not-me—and then we judge one pole to be "better" and the other to be "worse." Whenever we become attached to this judgmentalism, something "other" is always condemned in order that our egotism's delusional belief in itself as real—as well as its sense of itself as stable, secure, rational, masterful, substantial, and even immortal—can be endorsed.

The tyranny of malice results from this human compulsion to render judgments about everything that we consider "bad" or "wrong" . . . to live, to greater or lesser degree, in hatred of anything that threatens our delusions of security in "being right" . . . to bring harm upon whatever we consider "other" (and invariably also on ourselves) . . . and to act addictively with physical or emotional violence. Sooner or later, all this is entailed by the exercise of our judgmentalism. Even when we try sincerely and valiantly to be less malicious in our daily conduct—for example, by pursuing all sorts of moralizing ideologies, adhering to all sorts of "great values" or belief systems, and subscribing to all sorts of "higher" humanistic and religious beliefs—the very functioning of our judgmental mind continues to produce and reproduce the ubiquitous structure of our malice. Moralizing ideologies are a clever and cunning means by which our egotism justifies itself, and substantiates the delusional reality of its own existence.

Our egotism is addictively attached to the judgmentalism of

our chattering mind. So we struggle through our lives, coping with malice both internally and externally, and experiencing ourselves alienated from our own sexual-spiritual energies.

Human egotism is fear-based. It is terrified of the free-flow of our erotic energies, and chooses instead to live in the delusion that it could itself be secure and substantial. The judgmentalism of our chattering mind acts as if it could, by its incessant productivity, validate this sense of security and substantiality. Our egotism lives in the delusion that it could, by the compulsive repetitiousness of its judgmentalism, reign forever. By means of this attachment to itself—its attachment to its own judgmental faculties—our egotism temporarily wards off its own dissolution by obstructing the exuberance of erotic energies that flow within, through, and all around our human embodiment. In this manner, we struggle incessantly to refuse life's invitation to surrender our egotism to the supreme flow of the universe. Our egotism is terrified of us falling into alignment with the Sacred Unity, which is that of the truthfulness of Love.

## What is meditation?

Meditation is the spiritual practice that invites our egotism to surrender itself to the divinity of the lifeforce within us. This is the tantric way. It is the way of being that frees us from the incessant productivity of our judgmentalism. It is the process that dissolves our egotism and evaporates our attachment to its futile struggles and its delusionality. In this way, meditation accesses and opens us to the godliness that is the "light" in all that lives around us and within us, which is the supreme light of Love. Meditation is this process of living life on an existential path that realigns our being-in-the-world with the experience and the ethicality of the universe's supreme vibration. It is an intensely aware process of experiencing the present as the presence of what *is*. Meditation brings us into the reality of the here-and-now in a way that releases us from the customary and compulsive operation of our judgmental faculties, which are always referentially attached to the representation of pasts and futures. Meditation is not a refinement of our judgmentalism, but a releasing of our being from our imprisonment in the preoccupations of judging and doing. It is neither an act of "deep thought," nor an act of mindless, auto-hypnotic relaxation and silent stupefaction. Rather, meditation is a process of awareness—of a consciousness that is sometimes called "mindfulness"—that liberates us from our attachment to the chattering mind, and that emancipates our everyday experience from the tyranny of malice.

Meditation is profoundly dangerous to our egotism. To live in meditation is the most challenging path known to humanity, and the most courageous way to be. To live in meditation is to dwell adventurously in the timespace of releasing, expansion and openness. It is to live in the present and in the presence of our experience— instead of living in our egotism's representations of a past to which we hang back or a future to which we push forward. To dwell at this adventurous edge of life is to invite our egotism toward its dissolution, and to enter the realm of life's potential to bring us into joy, bliss, and ecstasy. As we live at our edge, we move into meditation, and as we do so we find that our experiences shift profoundly. We shift from conventional knowing, to unknowing, and then to mystical knowing.

Before meditation, our egotism is desperately attached to the "knowledge" accrued by its judgmentalism. By means of acquiring this knowledge, our egotism knows that it knows something, and therefore believes it knows that it itself exists. Our chattering mind chatters only by means of this conventional "wisdom." Our egotism is fundamentally a quite paranoid accretion of judgments generated by our social surroundings. Its "knowledge" is not only of science, but also of religion as well as cultural and personal myth. It is the knowledge inscribed in all our stories about our world and ourselves. It is the system of representations—of the various networks of languages, signs and meanings—in which we live. This has been called the "thetic" or "identitarian" world of representational thinking, in which we firmly believe that *"this is this,"* and that *"x"* can never be identical with *"not-x."* This is the world of all the logical and rhetorical devices by which we do things. It is a world sustained by what has been called the "compulsive repetitiousness" of our chattering mind.*

Most of us live mindlessly in this world just because it appears given to us "as is." However, when our thinking is turned against itself, as when we turn inwards to serious reflection and contemplation, we engage in a salutary critique of our own ideologies. The reflective turn in which we think about thinking— as is developed in philosophy, physics and psychoanalysis—tends to make us realize that everything we take to be the case is actually very much a matter of our representations. Reflection tends to erode our egotism's sense of certainty about itself. Neither logic nor rhetoric has firm foundations. Contemporary "postmodern" tendencies in the culture of western thinking—from the "new sciences" to deconstructive psychoanalysis—join ancient traditions of mystical vision in finding that there is ultimately neither security nor stability to be had in the domain of language and thought. Sooner or later, the logic and rhetoric with which our chattering mind "validates" its existence lead us to the abyss.

As we move into meditation, we come to realize that everything our egotism holds to be true is really quite arbitrary. What we had taken as "knowledge" is merely a matter of our egotism's representational construction. The "world" as we know it—in the conventional sense of knowing—is a matter of our belief that *"a is a"* and that *"a is not b."* Our chattering mind constructs a "world" of meanings for us based on the compulsive repetition of such representations. We live in this world of identities, positions, and

---

* If you would enjoy a scholarly exposition of these philosophical notions of the "identitarianism" of our mental functioning and of our egotism's "compulsive repetitiousness" (as well as a discussion of some of the assertions made about psychoanalysis in this essay), please consult my *Psychoanalysis and the Postmodern Impulse* (Baltimore, MD, Johns Hopkins University Press, 1993). But please also be mindful of Osho's teaching: Knowledge that is helpful at the time of our death is wisdom; knowledge that is not is scholarship!

stories—the delusional world of *māya*. This "world" we live in is founded both on categories—either/or, present/absent, good/bad, pleasure/pain, life/death, me/not-me—that we place in a hierarchy of "better" or "worse," and on a phenomenology that divides everything into past/present/future. This leaves us stranded in a delusional "present" that is always the *re*-presented present of pasts and futures, which do not exist here-and-now. As we move into meditation the bottom falls out of this edifice, and we fall into the abyss. Moving into meditation, we fall into the presence of reality. We fall into the realization of the void, the emptiness that pervades everything that *is* and *is not*.

When our egotism falls apart, we fall into unknowing as we come to realize the ecstatic emptiness of the here-and-now. Freed of all pasts and futures, meditation brings us into a timespace that is radically existential and experiential. We realize that this present is all that *is*, containing all possible "pasts" and "futures," and we realize that this here-and-now is joyously empty. It is the desire that moves all things, animating both being and nonbeing. It is "in" but not "of" the world, "in" but not "of" our own bodymind. Falling into meditation, we realize not only that everything is interconnected through the emptiness of this universal desire, but also that all we had once categorized as dichotomously separate is not. What is present is always already an absencing; what is absent is always already here-and-now. In our heart, we are one heart.

If we glimpse meditation but remain in the identitarian world of our egotism's representations, the meditator might appear nihilistic, merely detached from the conventional knowing of the world, and floating in arbitrariness. Life appears merely to become aleatory—as if we might as well conduct it by the throw of dice. But this unconventional freedom of "going with the flow" is not actually nihilism at all. Rather, it is the process of meditation moving us out of inauthentic "knowing." It is the process in which our egotism is deconstructed and dissolved, through transgression and transcendence. What might appear nihilistic is, sooner or later, the deep realization of Love.

For our egotism, Love is a catastrophe. So for our egotism to sustain itself, it is imperative that it keeps us out of the mystical depth and esoteric power of living in meditation. Our egotism is very clever and cunning in this enterprise. For example, it is a distractive trick of our egotism to imagine that "meditation" is some sort of special mental device or technique that might reinvigorate the productivity of our chattering mind.

We do not need a mat to meditate. We do not need a cabin by the ocean, or a hut in the Himalayas. We do not need candles, incense, or the chiming of temple bells. Nor do we need exotic wavelengths piped through high-tech equipment. We do not need training in the chanting of mantras, or in the contemplation of mandalas and other sacred images. We do not need psychedelics. Nor do we need to sequester ourselves in a monastery, shrine or temple. We do not need the authority of a priest, or even the blessing of a teacher.

It may be that, on occasion, such accoutrements and procedures are indeed helpful. But they are not essential. For meditation is not an intermittent event, nor is it a matter of mental trickery. Meditation is a life's journey, not an occasional trip. It is a process or method involving the letting go of our egotistic addiction, and a surrendering to the divine flow of our being. In this process, the appearance of techniques, tricks and "helpful" devices is usually indicative of our egotism's struggle to reassert itself.

Meditation is itself a movement of our being-in-the-world into a radically different timespace from that of our judgmental compulsivity, and as such we can fall into the divine spirit of meditation anytime and anywhere. So it is a deceit of our egotism to insist that meditation requires some special procedure in a special time or in a special space. To fall into the timespace of meditation is not a process that can be sequestered into twenty minutes or an hour a day. Rather, to fall into the timespace of Love is to live fully and methodically in the spirit of meditation. This is a process of living to be engaged in every moment of life itself. It is an adventurous holistic process, passionately and compassionately engaging every aspect of our existence.

Meditation is this process of wholly releasing ourselves from the business and busyness of our chattering mind, until the chattering becomes quiet and our egotism evaporates into bliss. As such, it is the way of our enlightening. It is the process of falling into the deep silence, the ecstatic emptiness, the Sacred Unity that infuses and underlies every moment of life itself. Living in meditation, we divest ourselves from the alienating preoccupations of our chattering mind, and surrender ourselves to blossom in the spirit of our compassionate witnessing.

## The Compassionate Witness

It is essential to cultivate our "Compassionate Witness." The essence of meditation is allowing ourselves to fall into the arms of this Beloved that is within us. This is the Beloved of our heart's desire. It is, so to speak, our individual moment of Holy Spirit, our access to the lifeforce that lives within us, the abundantly and exuberantly erotic energies that flow through us rendering our access to the Sacred Unity of Love.

Cultivating the Compassionate Witness stills the chattering mind, dissolves our egotism's attachment to itself, and thus eventually evaporates our egotism altogether, releasing us into the expansive opening of our being that is sometimes called "enlightenment."

We have said that our egotism forms itself fearfully by obstructing the abundance of the lifeforce, or *prāna*, that flows exuberantly within, through, and all around our bodymind. These obstructions become evident to us in all aspects of our bodymind. They occur in the structure and functioning of our mental activity as the compulsive repetitiousness of chattering thought patterns. And they occur concomitantly in the structure and functioning of our bodies, both as the physical inscription of memories in our connective tissues and as patterns of inhibition in our capacity for orgasmic ecstasy. We conduct ourselves in a manner that demonstrates how terrified we are of our potential to live heaven here-and-now on earth, to realize our divinity, and to open ourselves expansively to the godliness that is everywhere present in everything.

Our egotism is founded on our fear of the joyful flow of our erotic potential—precisely because its abundance and exuberance entails the deathful dissolution of our egotism.

This is why our egotism is so addictively attached to itself, which means that it is attached to the malicious judgmentalism of our chattering mind. And this is why we said that the problem of human malice arises whenever our erotic energies are blocked by our egotism's preoccupation with the judgmentalism of its own chattering mind, and that living in meditation—cultivating the Compassionate Witness within—is the only solution to this problem.

To find the Compassionate Witness, you are invited to try the following experiment:

*Stop!*
*Cease, here-and-now, whatever you are doing and thinking.*
*Freeze everything.*
*Instantly stop every mental and physical exertion!*

With *stopping*, we immediately notice a break in our attachment to our own physical being and to the chattering commotion of our own mental activity. We fall, at least briefly, into a new awareness. This awareness is a sort of "inactive-yet-alive-and-alert" condition of *witnessing* our bodymind. It is an awareness, or mindfulness, in which we are no longer fully identified with our physicality, and no longer so fully attached to all the identities, positions and stories, which incessantly preoccupy our everyday consciousness—a consciousness that is usually a sort of automated "unconsciousness."

This experiment of *stopping* allows us to experience momentarily a here-and-now that breaks our attachment to our identification with ourselves. This is a break with the chattering in which we incessantly re-present ourselves and our world to ourselves. This momentary break allows us, in a fresh here-and-now, to "step outside" and notice briefly our strenuous preoccupation with this "re-presenting"—the representational or judgmental activity in which we are characteristically immersed, with its medley of represented pasts and represented futures. In this brief breakage, we discover that we do not have to be totally preoccupied with the business and busyness of pretending to be ourselves. We do not have to be entirely identified with the productivity of our chattering mind.

In this experiment, we find an inner witness that allows us to be aware, without being identified and consumed by all our doing and thinking. We become slightly, and delightfully, strange to ourselves.

The experiment of *stopping* is just an experiment. Although we may only be able to be in this new awareness for a few milliseconds—before our chattering mind starts assessing things, and our body starts fidgeting—the experiment allows us to notice ourselves from a different timespace. This is the timespace of *being* rather than doing, acting and thinking. It is the timespace in which presence and absence are united in their difference—or *différance* as discussed by deconstructive philosophy. This is the dynamic process of presencing and absencing—which Buddhists point to as the *emptiness* that pervades all manifestations—and it is a timespace that is radically different from the time and space of all the pasts and futures that our chattering mind keeps representing to us. This timespace of the here-and-now is that of our inner witness. It is the timespace of spiritual awareness. It is the timespace of our sexual-spiritual energies.

Notice that the experiment of *stopping* was a break, rather than a change of pace. If we had merely taken an intermission in order to evaluate—for example, "Is my body posture good or bad? Was I just thinking something right or wrong?"—we would have remained in the realm of the chattering mind. We would have merely been engaged in a mode of reflective thinking that objectifies and judges the productivity of our chattering mind, and that is itself a product of our chattering mind. This is what some psychoanalysts have called the "observing ego." It has applications that can, on occasion, be helpful to us, but it is not equivalent to the cultivation of spiritual awareness.

Instead of observantly judging ourselves, the process of *stopping* invites us toward a deeper experience. It invites us to experience not the engagement of a higher order of thinking, but rather our potential to *be* in a process of spiritual awareness that is *otherwise* than the mechanics of doing, acting and thinking. We are discovering the witness within—a witness that is otherwise than judgmentalism, a witness that is inherently compassionate. This is the Beloved of our heart's universal desire.

Meditation has been described as a sort of process of "stepping outside and looking within." It is sometimes called "insight meditation" or *vipassanā*. Here the term "insight" means looking inwards compassionately, which is very different from the ordinary concept of "gaining insight"—as the objectifying formulation of narratives about something that is observed. Meditation is a "stepping outside" the representational world of our egotism, which is sustained by the compulsively repetitive judgmentalism of our chattering mind. It breaks with our egotism's addictive attachment to itself and is thus "outside" the representational world perpetuated by our chatter. Yet meditation takes us authentically deeper into ourselves, and in this sense it is a journey behind, beneath and beyond the mask of our chattering selves. It is a journey inside, a journey into silence, emptiness, and ecstasy. It is the discovery of our divine selves, a return to the godliness that is within every one of us. Meditation allows us to fall into the arms of the Beloved.

Egotism perpetuates our state of alienation from our own sexual-spiritual energies, our *prāna,* lifeforce, or divine sourcing. Meditation moves us out of the alienation of our egotism. It frees the lifeforce within us, and estranges us from the productivity of our egotism. It estranges us from all the identities, positions and stories that our chattering mind produces and reproduces about "me," about what is "other," and about the delusional "world" in which we commonly live. In this sense, meditation transmutes us from the state of alienation, into a dynamic process of estrangement. But in this estrangement from our egotism, we become authentically ourselves.

We begin to witness the machinations of our chattering mind—all the business and busyness, all the doing, acting and thinking, that characteristically preoccupy us. We witness our thrills and our disappointments, our humility and our pride, our sense of duty and our dishonor. We witness our preoccupation with matters of shame and humiliation, and of guilt and punishment. We witness our generosity and our possessiveness, our charity and our envy, jealousy, hostility, and anger. We witness how we dwell in memory and in anticipation. And we witness our fervor for domination, possession and control, our preoccupation with the manipulation of strategies, goals and outcomes. We witness how we debase "love" into a transactional exchange of emotional benefits and material commodities.

In meditation, we witness this hubbub, not to struggle against it judgmentally, and not to remedy it. Rather, we just witness it compassionately. That is, we witness our thoughts arising and subsiding, and we let them pass—without evaluating them, and without attaching ourselves to them. This process treats our thoughts and beliefs as if they were fluffy clouds in the sky—we witness their coming and going as they float by us. We witness them compassionately without attaching ourselves to their direction or outcome, without believing that we are them, without trying to make them go one way or another, and without trying to endorse some and repudiate others.

As we cultivate this Compassionate Witness within—or more accurately as we fall into our own compassionate witnessing, into the arms of the Beloved—our energies become unblocked. Our egotism's addictive attachment to itself loses its force. Obstructions in the flow of erotic energies within, through and around us, begin to dissolve. We become newly aware of whatever is here-and-now, as we experience presence authentically—without attachment to our judgmentalism. We enjoy life with equanimity, and experience a profound serenity that we had never thought possible.

As we release ourselves from our identification with our mind's chatter, we become aware of the abundant flow of the lifeforce that flows within, through, and around our embodiment. This awareness aligns us with the lifeforce, for our Compassionate Witness *is* pure *prāna.* Unlike the chattering mind, this mindfulness expresses our natural lifeforce, and is aligned with our erotic energies.

The sexual and spiritual sourcing of our embodiment is one. Meditation moves us out of our alienated state, into a joyous estrangement from our own egotism—an estrangement in which our erotic energies flow freely and our Compassionate Witness blossoms into fullness.

All this seems paradoxical and frightening to the mistaken logic and rhetoric of our egotism. For as meditation brings us into compassionate witnessing, we become more estranged from what psychologists call our egotism's "character structure" or "personality," but we become more individually, intensely, authentically, and exuberantly alive. The movement out of our egotistic alienation from our sexual-spiritual sourcing, toward a dynamic estrangement from our own chattering mind, is a momentum in which we become passionately engaged in life, yet also compassionately detached from the turbulence of our chattering mind. We become fully and joyfully engaged in life, yet no longer attached to our own egotism.

Compassionately witnessing our egotism's struggles and the compulsive futility of our chattering mind, we become aware. The cultivation of our Compassionate Witness is our spiritual enlightening. This is naturally invigorating. As soon as we loosen our attachment to what we once grasped as ourselves, we come to enjoy life completely, without separation from its flow, its esoteric depth and its mystical power. Cultivation of our Compassionate Witness—falling into the arms of our Beloved—drains our egotism of its forcefulness, and casts us into the dynamic flow of life itself. The *prāna* accessed through our compassionate witnessing aligns us with what we had lost. It returns us to the truthfulness of Love that is the supreme flow of the universe—and it brings us into awareness of the lifeforce that unites what our chattering mind represented as the dichotomy of its "life" and "death."

For our spiritual enlightening, the only crucial question for our particular life's journey concerns how we are to stop our mind's judgmental chattering, emancipate ourselves from our egotism, enjoy our sexual-spiritual energies, and cultivate our Compassionate Witness. The question of living in meditation—the only question that attends to our spiritual enlightening—concerns how we may fall into the arms of the Beloved, how we may relinquish suffering to become happy and free.

We owe to Osho, and all the spiritually enlightened teachers who preceded him, a wonderful array of suggestions for the practice of "active" or "dynamic" meditation. We have already mentioned one to start with—the practice of *stopping!* However, the Compassionate Witness may also be cultivated methodically in any number of other ways. We may fall into the arms of the Beloved, and out of our egotism, anytime and anywhere. Our enlightening is for here-and-now, and cannot be postponed to there-and-then. We may methodically access our potential to live in meditation by attending to the awareness of our breathing, moving, vibrating, and orgasming—and then we come to meditate in the dance of life itself, for in our lovemaking with life, we access Holy Spirit, the lifeforce that is the sourcing of our divinity.

## Breathing Meditation

What is our life? We miss the spiritual dimension whenever we think of our life as consisting of all the identities, positions, and stories that our chattering mind pronounces about "me." However much our life may appear to have a beginning, middle and end, it is not contained within the representations of our egotism. Indeed, the identities, positions and stories that we assume about ourselves are merely ephemeral constructions, the fabric of our egotism's insistence that we live life in delusion. Life is not really a narrative, told and retold by our chattering mind. Rather, in meditation, we come to know our spiritual life as *prāna*.

We come to know the truthfulness of the universe as the ecstatic emptiness of Love. This is a knowledge to which words can only point inadequately. This is the supreme truthfulness that is unthinkable and inexpressible for our chattering mind—a truthfulness that is intimated to our egotism in the terror of its own dissolution.

From the cradle to the grave, our embodiment is a magnificent conduit for the lifeforce. This is what our life *is*. As the most ancient scriptures hinted, *Tat Tvam Asi,* "That-Thou-Art!" Godliness is absolute and everywhere, as the Sacred Unity of the lifeforce in which all matters of life and death are conjoined. Spiritually, this is what each of our particular lives actually *is*, most authentically and profoundly: A pulse or vibration in the entire dancing diaphragm of the divine universe.

Our breathing is the most obvious manifestation of the movement of *prāna* through our embodiment. It is the clearest and simplest evidence that we are alive! So meditation begins and ends simultaneously in our breathing. The awareness of breathing thus becomes foundational to our practice of meditation.

When our mind chatters, we tend to breathe automatically, without awareness. Governed by our egotism, our breath is conditioned and constrained to follow the vicissitudes of our chattering mind. But as we fall into meditation, our mindfulness follows our breathing. This process shifts us out of our "unconscious" state, in which our breath seems to follow the repetitive logic and rhetoric of our chattering mind. It shifts us into the awareness of our breathing. The practice of inviting our mindfulness to rest on the pulsing of our breath is the fundamentally significant move into meditation.

We know that, when we are anxious, our breath tends to become sharp, shallow, and constricted in our thoracic cavity. It is well known, among healers, that deliberately deepening the breath—so that we focus its momentum on the expansion of the entire diaphragm—usually has a calming influence on the preoccupations of our chattering mind. We can notice here how, in ordinarily "unconscious" states, we readily allow our chattering mind to dictate—that is to condition and constrain—the momentum of our breath. To live in meditation is to invite our awareness to follow our breathing.

There are many different ways of breathing, and many different practices of *prāṇāyāma*—of working and playing with the mindfulness of our breath. One helpful practice is as follows. Seated in a comfortable upright posture, we attend to the deepening of our breath. Closing our eyes helps us to focus inward. We inhale deeply, from the bottom upwards, filling our diaphragm as our navel pushes outward, and then filling our thoracic cavity by expanding our chest all the way up to the collarbones. We exhale deeply, from the top downwards, emptying our thoracic cavity as our chest muscles relax, and then emptying our diaphragm as our navel relaxes inward. We focus ourselves on this inner movement of our breath. As we settle ourselves into this relaxed breathing, we invite our attention to rest on the sensation just below our nostrils, where we may feel the air gently moving in and out. This sensation becomes very subtle and focused. We invite the cultivation of our mindfulness through this subtlety and focus.

Without practice, most of us can allow our attention to settle on this gentle rhythm for only a few seconds. Then our chattering mind grabs our attention, overruns the practice, and displaces our mindfulness—we have been kidnapped! Our chattering mind will readily divert our attention to a preoccupation with some other sensation, or to a deliberation over some past or future event. When this distractibility occurs, the practice of meditation is neither to indulge nor to struggle against the chattering mind. The stress of opposition only reinforces the activity of the chattering mind. Both compliance and defiance strengthen our egotism. To struggle against chatter is to chatter all the more. Rather, when chatter occurs, our practice is simply and gently to invite our attention to return to the subtle sensation of the presence of our breath flowing in and out, just below our nostrils. We may experiment with this mindful breathing—and with our chattering mind's resistance to it—as a foundational approach to meditation.

The tone of such a practice is that we do not judge or condemn our chattering mind for insisting on doing what it knows best. Rather, we appreciate it even while relinquishing its grip over us. So in this practice, we become—or rather, we find ourselves as—

our Compassionate Witness. Thought forms, including all interrupting sensations and seemingly urgent deliberations, amalgamate and dissipate. We witness them, and let them pass. Returning ourselves to the mindfulness of our breathing, we bid our chattering preoccupations goodbye. As our awareness rests on the subtle focus of breathing, our thoughts, feelings and fantasies become like clouds in the sky. We witness them compassionately, but we decline to get attached to them.

This is the basic exercise of *vipassanā* meditation, in which some spiritual seekers choose to discipline themselves for hours and days. Falling into this breathing meditation as often as we are able—throughout our daily lives—has wonderfully beneficial consequences in every aspect of our being, for the challenge and the power of this practice are immense. In breathing meditation, we may take ourselves to the edge of our existence, for our "edge" is always sensed by our breath, and by the entire momentum of our *prāna.* To hang back fearfully from our edge is always to consign ourselves to becoming less magnificent than we truly are, to constrict ourselves in a manner that is very conducive to the ambitions of our egotism. To try to push ourselves beyond this edge, forcing ourselves beyond our natural capacity, is also very conducive to the ambitions of our egotism and—despite its appearance of bravado—is a fearful act that furthers our sexual-spiritual alienation, inevitably causing us to recoil into constriction. But to live at our edge is to live the sexual-spiritual adventure of meditation, in which we take ourselves back to our breathing and to the edge of our existence whenever we sense that we are hanging back from it or forcing ourselves against it. In this way, breathing meditation enables us to live adventurously in the timespace of releasing, expansion and openness. We gain equanimity and serenity in the face of all our difficulties, and in the face of all our suffering. We become supple and filled with joy.

The awareness of our breathing is resisted mightily by our egotism, which volunteers to pay attention to respiration only when it is in crisis. This is because the awareness of our breath not only dispels our mind's chatter, but also brings us face-to-face with the deathfulness by which we live. Our egotism will instigate crises in order to avert this confrontation.

Consider this: As we become aware of the rhythm of inhaling and exhaling, the movement of the in-breath and of the out-breath connotes our aliveness. The momentary "cessation" of the breath—that is, between the in-breath becoming the out-breath, and between the out-breath becoming the in-breath—invites us to "know" whatever is neither life nor death, and both life and death. We are not referring to the absurd heroics of "holding one's breath," but rather to a cessation that is entirely natural, and that occurs with every breath. And this is not a "knowing" that our chattering mind can formulate, name, or speak. Rather, in this moment of "neither breathing nor not-breathing," we experience the void that lies behind, beneath or beyond all our thoughts and beliefs, and yet is the void pervading all that *is*. This void connotes the deathfulness that is enfolded within every moment of life itself—the deathfulness without which there is no life. This is like the abyss that we may experience briefly between one thought form and another, in which we open ourselves to the deathfulness that animates all that *is*. This opening is an expanding of ourselves into our spiritual being. Between breaths and between thoughts, we glimpse ourselves as different and far greater than our egotism. We glimpse ourselves as more than our egotism can bear. This brief syncopation is actually a moment in which we expand into an openness that is outside of our egotism. As such it is the harbinger of our egotism's dissolution.

In this way, mindfulness of the process of breathing brings us to the margins of life and death. More accurately, the awareness of our breathing brings us to the realization that we are only alive because we are, throughout the course of our lives, always at this "margin." That is, in the awareness of our breath, we realize that "life" and "death" are not dichotomous timeframes in a storyline. Rather, life and death are always enfolded into each other, throughout every moment that is here-and-now. Just as presence and absence are not binary opposites, for every presence contains

its own absencing, and an ecstatic emptiness infuses the apparent
manifestations of presence and absence.

In becoming aware of our breathing, we confront how the
liveliness of our life depends upon this inescapable deathfulness
that pervades every present moment of our being-in-the world.
Breathing meditation brings us rapidly to this realization.

This confrontation with the deathfulness of life spells disaster
for our egotism—which struggles to sustain the delusion that its
representations of life are stable, secure, rational, masterful,
substantial, immortal, and so on. As if to avert this existential and
experiential realization of the deathfulness of life—as if to avert its
own dissolution into the flow of ecstatic emptiness that pervades
and yet is also behind, beneath, and beyond the manifestations of
life and death—our egotism instigates crises to keep us out of the
awareness of our breath. This is why the practice of breathing
meditation is so challenging and so powerful. It is also why
meditation requires courage, and is the greatest adventure known
to humankind.

In the practice of breathing meditation—or any meditation
method that is engaged—disturbing thoughts and feelings will
inevitably, sooner or later, erupt. Painful memories of our
traumatization are frequently reactivated, coming to the surface of
our consciousness in ways that may be alarming. As if resisting its
own calming, our chattering mind may initiate stormy outbursts
and catharses. Our fears of emotional breakdown and of "going
mad" are easily evoked. We all have the potential to pass through
our terror if we continue to relax into the awareness of our breathing.
To surpass suffering, we cultivate the Compassionate Witness that
watches all the manifestations of our fears as they arise, attempt to
snatch us away from meditation, and then pass on as we thank
them goodbye.

Breathing meditation aligns us with the flow of the lifeforce.
So we may anticipate that its regular practice will sooner or later
release the blockages our egotism has maintained in our bodies
and our minds. Such releasing purges us. The challenge and the
power of breathing meditation are precisely in this process by which

our Compassionate Witness is cultivated, and we become aligned with the *prāna* that is the holiness of our being-in-the-world.

## Dancing Meditation

The indissoluble unity of the liveliness and the deathfulness of our lives is a dance. This is the moving and vibrating of Holy Spirit within us. We dance on this "margin" of life and death that is the reality of the presencing of the present. Only the delusionality of our egotism believes life to be otherwise than this.

Dancing—the entire process of casting our bodymind into the flow of whatever *is*—is the essence of meditation. The secret of life is to dance through it. To dance is to relinquish our egotistic ambition to control life by attempting to dominate others and ourselves. Rather we allow the dance of life to lead us. Whatever we may be doing can be surrendered to this dance. This means that we allow ourselves to become completely immersed in the dance yet, in the same moment, we also witness ourselves being swept into this flow of what *is*. And, as has been said, this compassionate witnessing is our authentic, spiritual "self," for it is the heart of our being.

We may be swept away in the rhythm of music. We may be creating artwork by allowing the muse to express herself through us, or we may be engaged in the whimsy of childlike playfulness. We may be entranced in the chanting of mantras, or we may be absorbed in the contemplation of a mandala. Whatever activity we are engaged in, we allow the momentum of its dance to carry us out of ourselves. We invite our egotism to surrender to the dance that comes from without. We allow ourselves to be completely, passionately immersed in the activity, yet also compassionately witnessing our immersion.

It is mistaken to believe that to meditate we must remain physically immobile. In the movement of our embodiment there is a natural fluidity and rhythm that can carry us toward the dissolution of our egotistic judgmentalism. Regrettably, many of us have lost our awareness of this wisdom of our bodies—this natural fluidity and rhythm. So meditation is needed to allow us to listen to this mystical intelligence. We can cultivate our Compassionate Witness and be aware of the rhythm of our breathing while our body moves through everyday activities. Walking, running, jumping, swimming, performing yogic poses . . . may all be performed as meditation. They must be engaged, not as the outcomes of our chattering mind's ambition to govern our lives, but rather as the dance of *prāna* into which we can surrender.

The naturalness and spontaneity of bodily movement actually stills the chattering mind. Dancing with aliveness involves moving and vibrating our entire bodymind. It is generated by the dynamics of our subtle erotic energies. Such dancing is the essential feature of meditation. Again, the crucial issue for these practices is that the entire bodymind follows the dance, rather than the "dance" be orchestrated by the chattering mind. We move into dancing meditation as soon as we relinquish the law and order of choreography and regimentation—as soon as we relinquish evaluation and expectation, for our dancing cannot be guided by rules, regulations, or goals. We move into dancing meditation as soon as we allow ourselves the spontaneity of surrender to the flow that comes from without, and allow our being to witness compassionately our surrender to the rhythm of this dancing.

There are many different ways of falling into the dance of life, and many different practices of dancing meditation. One helpful practice is as follows. We locate ourselves in an undisturbed situation, with an upright posture and room to move—perhaps with our eyes closed, or half-closed to enhance our focus inwards. We take some deep breaths, and invite our attention initially to rest on the momentum of our breathing. We may then also take a few moments to encourage our chattering mind to let go its preoccupations, as well as a few minutes to shake loose any stiffness or tightness that we feel in our limbs. Then we invite our mindful attention to listen to the rhythm of whatever tunefulness is in the air. This may actually be a piece of music—but not a piece to which our chattering mind can immediately attach some choreographic scheme—or it may be the sound of the waves on a beach, the chirping of birds, the feel of a gentle breeze, or the swaying of trees. Whatever "external stimulus" we may appear to be listening to, we are really inviting ourselves to attend to the pulsations of the lifeforce that flows all around us. And as we attune to this "music," we allow our entire bodymind to be absorbed in it, such that we find ourselves moving to its flow. We fall into a complete immersion in the momentum that sweeps us in its embrace, and we compassionately witness our being swept away in this immersion.

As with breathing meditation, our egotism will resist this spiritual practice with all its might. Typically, our chattering mind will interrupt our immersion by evaluating the "success" of our "dance technique," or distracting us with other irrelevancies. And as with all meditation practice, we do not fight against our egotism. Rather, we witness ourselves being kidnapped by our chattering mind, and we gently invite ourselves back into the dance. This is a basic practice of dancing meditation, in which great enjoyment is to be found. Falling into this meditation as often as we are able—throughout the course of every day—has wonderfully beneficial consequences in every facet of our lives. We become serene and supple, as our egotism is released, and we become alive as we release ourselves to the flow of *prāna* around us so as to experience fully and joyfully the flow of *prāna* that dances within us.

Osho's "active" or "dynamic" meditations offer specific suggestions as to how we may lose our egotism by immersing ourselves in the natural and spontaneous rhythm of life's momentum. Some of these suggestions are methodical, in the sense that they seem to invite our various "chakras" into the dance one by one. The chakras are like energy vortices or channels that run through our embodiment, aiding us in becoming aware of the flow of *prāna* that ripples and undulates throughout our being. With these methods, we learn to dance by attuning to the specific rhythm of particular vibrations. We learn to dance in ways that release our patterns of blockage, obstruction and repetition—freeing us to become a clearer conduit for the flow of divine energies. All these methods of dynamic meditation share the essential practice of surrendering to the moving and vibrating power of our *prāna,* and inviting ourselves to become aware of ourselves as we flow in this power. To meditate we need only allow our bodymind to follow the moving and vibrating energies of the lifeforce that flows within us, through us, and all around us. We need to relinquish our egotism's repetitive pattern of treating our bodily actions as if they were the instrument of its own mistaken or delusional sense of law and order. A natural and spontaneous immersion in the power of the lifeforce within us requires that we release ourselves from the imperatives and the governance of our egotism. We allow ourselves to flow into the invitation of our erotic energies. In the moving and vibrating of our bodymind, we cultivate our Compassionate Witness. The natural spontaneity of moving and vibrating with the flow of whatever *is* allows our chattering mind to fall into the stillness of a deep spiritual silence, and the preoccupations of our egotism to evaporate.

This is the essence of dancing meditation. It is a sexual-spiritual experience, in which the joyous sensuality of our being-in-the-world again invites the transgression and the transcendence of our egotistic interests. Meditation is always a mobilization of our erotic energies, a realignment of our being with the flow of the universe, and dancing meditation facilitates this spiritual process.

## Lovemaking Meditation

There are a thousand and one ways of moving and vibrating into meditation. Again we may notice three inseparably entwined characteristics that they all share. They gently unsettle our egotism, and invite its dissolution. They cultivate the *prāna* of our Compassionate Witness. And they celebrate life's Holy Spirit, which involves all the erotic energies of our entire bodymind. Breathing and dancing meditation, in all its many modalities, is an erotic performance that dissipates the anti-sexual and anti-spiritual constitution of our chattering mind, releasing us from our imprisonment in obstructions, resistances, blocks and hindrances.

Meditation is always a matter of sexual-spiritual practice, of dancing, and of lovemaking with the holiness of the lifeforce.

The orgasming of lovemaking is the culmination of these erotic practices. Orgasming is the rippling, undulating momentum of energies through our bodymind. It is a freeing of Holy Spirit within and through us—a release in which we become the conduit of the divine, and we experience the heaven-on-earth that is always already all around us. It is a delusion of our judgmental mind to imagine that heaven and earth are dichotomous categories, and in the process of orgasming we *know* this to be true—even though we cannot explain it. Only human egotism—our terror of hardship, loss, and death—keeps us in suffering and out of happiness. Heaven and earth are here-and-now in a timespace that is one-and-the-same. Only the edifice of our egotism blinds us to this.

Our lovemaking, surrendering us into orgasming, intimates our enlightening. For in the momentum in which lovemaking sweeps us away orgasmically, we experience joy, bliss, and ecstasy. In a way that we cannot articulate, we experience our potential to live heaven here-and-now on earth, unimpeded by the conditions and constraints of our judgmental mind.

It is a mistake to think—as our egotism would have us do—that we "have an orgasm," as if it were an experience we can possess, or as if it were a mechanical procedure under the governance of our chattering mind. When our chattering mind tells us that it can arrange for us to "have an orgasm," we miss the deeper spiritual flow of orgasming itself. For orgasming is not just one sort of physical event among many. Rather, it is an all-embracing sexual-spiritual process. An "orgasm" may have gross behavioral and physiological concomitants, but it is essentially a transportation and transmutation of the subtle sexual-spiritual energies that run through our embodiment. Orgasming is a process of releasing ourselves into the spontaneous and natural flow of the energies of our lifeforce.

Orgasming may be initiated—or appear to be initiated—from any part of the bodymind, for we are exuberantly sensual creatures.

However, as our orgasming intensifies, it sweeps our entire bodymind into the abundance of its flowing and overflowing momentum. It throws us "out of our heads" and into the joyous reality of our bodies, genitals and hearts. As its momentum deepens, orgasming brings our chattering mind into silence, dissolves our sense of separateness, and moves us into the natural processes of joy, bliss, and ecstasy. Lovemaking is this orgasming—whether with ourselves, with human partners, or with the aliveness of dolphins, trees, flowers, and rivers—and lovemaking is the quintessential spiritual practice.

It is also a mistake to think—as our egotism would have us do—that lovemaking is some sort of interpersonal transaction of our egotism, or that "love" is some sort of negotiation of emotional benefits or material commodities. Love is not a "relationship" in the conventional sense. Rather, it is the exuberant expression of the divine interconnectedness of all beings. Lovemaking—and the opening, expansive releasing of orgasming—offers us the enjoyment of the lifeforce in the process of our egotism's evaporation. So lovemaking is not a goal-oriented task, not a strategy of work that is part of our chattering mind's ambition. It has been a mistake, promoted by many psychoanalysts and sexologists, to imagine that the pleasures of lovemaking lie in the repetition of sensually "positive" patterns of interaction, or that it is follows a physical and emotional pattern that has previously been judged "satisfying." Rather, it is a process of casting ourselves into the playfulness of the universe. The pleasures of lovemaking lie in the breaking of repetitious patterns, the freeing of our energies into the dance of the universe, the delicious breaching of our prior patterns of performance. Lovemaking is a freeing of ourselves from our egotism. It is a releasing of ourselves to the dance of life. Lovemaking is the aware experience of sharing the energies of the lifeforce, and it is the awareness that, in our hearts, we are all one heart. It is not so much about affectionate sentiments or altruistic acts—which are all too readily recruited to our judgmental mind's struggle to justify itself. Rather, to lovemake is to share joyously in the erotic energies of the divine, the energies that connect us all intimately. To lovemake orgasmically—that is, to move together mindfully conjoined by the flow of erotic energies—is to live in meditation.

Lovemaking always "starts" with the self. That is, there is no lovemaking until we are prepared to cast our own egotism into the flow of lovemaking that is always already there available to us, at every time and in every place. The erotic spirit of lovemaking "starts" with our relinquishing the shame, guilt, and fearfulness that keeps us separate from the sexual-spiritual energies that flow within us, through us, and all around us. Although the orgasmic mobilization of erotic energies may be initiated from any part of our bodymind, our genitals often invite us to the immediate access of this mobilization. As we have said, the glories of our genitals are the altar for spiritual practice.

Living in meditation, our genitals are to be celebrated—revered and cherished for the conduit they offer to our divinity. Not only does such worship of the genitals free us from the shame and guilt that perpetuates our spiritual blockages, but the genitals also offer us the most powerful way of accessing, intensifying, mobilizing, and becoming aware of the erotic energies that flow within us. To arouse the energies of our genitals in the meditation of lovemaking is to awaken our divinity, inviting these energies to move through our chakras, until our entire bodymind becomes a vibrating conduit for Holy Spirit, with our erotic momentum rippling and undulating from our root to our crown, connecting us with the entirety of the universe.

There are many different ways of lovemaking in meditation, and many different ways of inviting ourselves into the flow of orgasmic pleasuring. For example, settling ourselves in a serene location, we may wish to shake loose any constriction we feel in our body. And we may also wish to take a few moments to perform a ritual of our own creation that serves to invite our chattering mind to let go its preoccupations and to allow us to enjoy fully the pleasures that are our birthright. Then, attending foremost to the deepening, relaxed rhythm of our breathing, we start gently to caress any part of ourselves, and we invite our mindful attention to rest on whatever sensations occur. If we are lovemaking solo, we attune ourselves to the minutiae of sensual pleasure occurring within. If we are lovemaking with a partner, we attune ourselves both to the sensuality within, and also equally to the sensuality of our partner, in whatever way this may be expressed and experienced by us. As we attune to this pleasuring, and as we allow our access to it to intensify, we become completely immersed in the sensuality and passion of feelings in the here-and-now, and we witness compassionately the presence of an exuberant joyfulness of erotic movement that is within us, within our partners, circulating through us, and in everything around us.

Whether we are experiencing a gentle brushing sensation on our arm, a warmth in our thoracic cavity, an intense charge within our genitals, or the depth of our partner's gaze, we are inviting ourselves to become attuned to the flow of the lifeforce within our bodymind, as well as to the flow of the lifeforce that circulates between us and our partners. As we attend to this erotic energy, we fall into its embrace and we witness compassionately the joy, bliss, and ecstasy of being in this flow. Erotic energy is inherently ecstatic. That is, its wonderful mobility takes us out of the repetitions in which we are stuck. Erotic energy takes us out of the obstructions, hindrances, resistances, and blockages that constitute the edifice of our egotism. It sweeps into joyous oblivion all our identities, positions, and stories—all our business and busyness. The ecstasy of our erotic momentum evaporates these incessant preoccupations of our chattering mind, casting us into the presence of reality—the presence of Holy Spirit.

As such, our egotism cannot tolerate the spiritual cultivation of our erotic being-in-the-world. At its very foundations, our egotism stands against our sexuality—so, as with breathing and dancing meditations, it will do anything to keep us out of authentic erotic pleasuring. Understanding all erotic energy to be a fundamental threat to its sense of stability and security, our egotism will try to turn sexuality into mere "sexiness." It will shroud our erotic nature in shame and guilt. It will arrange for the repression, suppression, inhibition or compulsivity of our erotic desire.

These anti-sexual and anti-spiritual ambitions of our egotism are evidenced in very specific ways as we approach orgasming. For example, our chattering mind may close down our sensual arousal, may preoccupy us with a "nonsexual fantasy," or may entertain us with a "sexual fantasy" that serves to distract us away from the awareness of the sensual flow of *prāna* that blossoms within us, through us, and all around us. As with other modes of meditation, our practice is not to judge these distractions, but rather to allow them to pass by, inviting ourselves to bring our mindful attention back to the sensual flow that is within us, and that circulates through our partners and ourselves. Again, we do not fight the ambitions of our egotism. Rather, we simply do not allow ourselves to become attached to them. We witness ourselves being kidnapped away from our erotic enjoyment, and we gently invite ourselves back to the dancing flow of energy that is our pleasuring.

As we develop lovemaking as meditation, as we allow ourselves to become immersed in the flow of erotic energies within us, we discover the magnificent power of orgasming. The process of orgasming involves our awareness of a rippling, undulating flow of energy within our bodymind. We find that the secret of enhancing our orgasming is always a matter of releasing ourselves to the naturalness of our breathing, our moving, and our vibrating with sound. Orgasming is the natural expressiveness of our releasing and opening ourselves to the expansiveness of our erotic energies. Breath, movement, and sounding out our vibrations are the keys to intensifying our lovemaking into the dance of its orgasmic potential. As orgasming intensifies, our energy sparkles from root to crown. Falling into this meditation as often as we are able—throughout every moment of our daily lives—is a profoundly and miraculously beneficial healing for every aspect of our bodymind. Sexual healing is the essence of living life in Love, of living prayerfully in meditation.

Lovemaking is the sacred act of enjoyment—of finding the joy in any and every manifestation of our lives. Meditation in lovemaking—within ourselves, between our partners, and with the universe—means that we move deeper into our erotic nature with the awareness of our Compassionate Witness. We move deeper into our sexual-spiritual being, not as the mindlessness of "sex acts" performed as a thrill orchestrated by our egotism, but as the mindfulness of the abundance and exuberance of the lifeforce that runs within us, through us, and all around us. With the cultivation of our Compassionate Witness, pleasuring becomes the focus of our meditation. Contrary to what many philosophers have theorized, pleasure lies in the mobilization of these sexual-spiritual energies. It is generated in our breaking with the compulsively repetitious patterns of thought and action that are the edifice of our egotism. Pleasuring is the moving, vibrating, dancing of our erotic energies. It is our major access to awareness of the lifeforce within us, and our path for finding the joy in any and every manifestation of our lives. This is the prayerfulness of our lovemaking and of our orgasming by which we find what is always already here-and-now in the present, our capacity to live in the ecstasy of meditation, our potential to live in the divinity of Holy Spirit.

## Shifting Experiences

Living in meditation changes us profoundly, such that we can never go back. It is the process of our enlightening. This is an ethical path, concordant with the five beautiful intentions that structure all spiritual practice in the Buddhist tradition. So perhaps the simplest way to move into a life of meditation is commit to these intentions: To revere life; To respect belongingness; To celebrate the sanctity of our passion; To express our truthfulness; To honor the temple of our bodymind.

To try following these precepts without meditation—that is, to make these five beautiful intentions into yet another moralizing ideology or belief system for our judgmental mind to wrestle with— not only misses the heart of these intentions, it is also impossibly arduous. Fundamentally, these five intentions are a calling that our egotism can neither stand nor withstand. The challenging adventure of this ethicality calls us into meditation. To be ethical, we need to meditate. There is no ethicality without lovemaking.

In a sense, one both can and cannot prepare for the life of meditation. We may begin by honoring the temple of our bodymind. For example, we may attend diligently to whatever we ingest, whether in our diet or in the panorama of stimuli that we are bombarded with daily; and we may attend diligently to whatever we expel, whether as unneeded materials from our body and our lifestyle, or as the ways in which we express ourselves in the world. These attentions are, in a certain sense, ethical acts of preparation. We may also consider all the methods that can contribute to the freeing of our "body" and our "mind"—while recognizing both that this is a false distinction used here merely as a heuristic, and that one type of method cannot be beneficial without the other. Let us mention some methods that may be helpful.

In terms of the "body," there are methods of bodywork that contribute to releasing the various patterns of blockage and constriction that we hold in our energy flow. These are the blockages and constrictions that we have acquired through the history of our emotional and physical traumatizations. For example, there are methods of massage, such as "rolfing," that directly confront our connective tissues in those locations where our muscular-skeletal system is no longer loose and limber. The entire medley of yoga practices that have been developed since Patanjali also serves in this emancipation. The real intent of *hatha* yoga—the practice of physical poses, accompanied by mindfulness of the breath—is not that we acquire the ability to contort ourselves into pretzel poses. In themselves, such accomplishments are not germane. The authentic intent of yogic discipline is not to achieve feats of physical or mental prowess, but rather to develop an avenue into meditation. The intent of a genuine yogic practice is always profoundly spiritual. It is both to release hindrances and resistances to the flow of *prāna* within us, and to cultivate our serene awareness of this flow of the lifeforce within us. All yoga is an aspect of tantra. If practiced well, yoga will always move us into the life of meditation.

In terms of the "mind," the methods of dynamic psychotherapy—principally the deconstructive methods of psychoanalytic healing—can be invaluable in releasing the diverse patterns of compulsively repetitious thought forms that variously obstruct the free-flow of our energy. These obstructions are longstanding schemes of thinking, feeling, acting, and negotiating relationships, that form the edifice of our egotism, and that have been acquired through the history of our emotional and physical traumatizations. The obstructions are evident in our attachment to all the stories by which we live—the manner in which our egotism governs our life by what has been called the "narratological imperative." Governed by our chattering mind, we live in fantasy, story, and delusion—the world of *māya*. Sometimes our egotism needs to be repaired before it can be released, and this is where the healing of psychotherapy—and of shamanic energy processes—can help us toward living life in meditation.

The real intent of psychoanalytic healing, for example, is not to re-attach ourselves to the stories of our personal history, nor to attach ourselves to explanations as to why these stories are so. The real intent of psychoanalytic healing is not to arrive at some sort of "new and improved" narrative as to how we should live. Rather, it is to release us from our compulsive attachment to living in stories, and thus to remobilize the spiritual desire of our erotic energy. If practiced well, dynamic psychotherapy liberates us from our resistances to the lifeforce, and cultivates our awareness of this flow within us—if practiced well, psychoanalysis will always move us into the life of meditation.

Care is needed in all these endeavors, for there are spiritual traps. Bodywork, yoga, and psychoanalysis can all become impediments to living in meditation. We can easily become attached to the very method that we initially engaged as a preparatory aid. Incessant preoccupation with bodywork can become an avoidance of the enjoyment of the body. Seemingly endless preoccupation with explanations of the history of our traumatizations can become an avoidance of the enjoyment of life itself. For example, some people become stuck on psychotherapy. They become so addicted to this method of elaborating and explaining the stories by which they live that they never let go their attachment to story-telling. We easily become enamored of the procedure and process of these methods. And instead of helpful phases in our moving toward meditation, they become recruited to our egotism's ambition to hold fast to itself. Such "preparations"—and procrastinations engineered by our chattering mind—are themselves the most devious means of obstruction.

There is another sense in which there is no preparation for living in meditation. Rather, we meditate and it just happens. Perhaps we really have only a single meaningful choice in life—a choice we make in every moment that we breathe. The choice is whether to live our life fully and passionately as the spiritual adventure that it is, or to avoid the liveliness of life by alienating ourselves from our erotic spirit, by preoccupying ourselves with matters of material gain and loss, and by investing ourselves in moralizing ideologies, belief systems, and the opinions of others.

The meditator often appears unconventional. We become indifferent to social and cultural mores, the rules and regulations that codify behavior and serve to reproduce the delusional "world" inhabited by our egotism. In meditation, we move from "knowing" the world as our egotism constructs it, through unknowing, and into *knowing* the mystical wisdom that is bathed in the Sacred Unity of Love. Transgression and transcendence are ways toward the deconstruction and dissolution of our egotism. So, for example, in meditation, we may disrobe, we play naked, and we dance our way out of shame, guilt, and anxiety. Refusing the delusions of separateness, we may touch, and invite the touch of, everything that comes before us. We lovemake with ourselves, and with all the creatures of the universe. We worship the beauty and the energy of our genitals. We lovemake with strangers, greeting them as a gift from the beyond. We may lovemake in cemeteries and cremation grounds, celebrating the lifefulness of "death," and experiencing the deathfulness of our erotic life. In pleasure, and in the experiences of hardship, pain and loss, we always celebrate life, embracing

fully and joyfully the inherent deathfulness within it. We dance—
endlessly and passionately with our entire being—and we break
with all the rules and regulations that would stifle our dancing.
We perform these practices so as to *be* rather than do—to get
ourselves "out of our heads," and into the alliance of our genitals,
our entire bodymind, and our hearts. This is the "craziness" of
spiritual wisdom. These transgressions go beyond being a mere
critique of stultifying convention, for they are neither concerned
with conventionality nor with unconventionality. Rather, breaking
the rules and regulations of our egotism is the way of
transcendence—the silencing of our judgmental mind. It is the
prayerful way of inviting our fearful egotism to evaporate—this is
the tantric path of living in meditation.

Our whole experience of life shifts with meditation. We move
from knowing—or, at least, believing that we know—as well as
from all the business and busyness of doing, to simply being. Once
preoccupied with domination, conquest, and with the control of
our lives, we now long only to surrender to the lifeforce itself. We
relinquish our investment in possessing, to find the joy of belonging.
We let go evaluation in order to celebrate in appreciation. We let
go all judgmental discrimination, to practice spiritual discernment.
We break with all that is merely habitual, to revel in spontaneity.
We free ourselves of all shame and guilt, addressing the
contingencies and vicissitudes of life fearless and without anxiety.
We free ourselves of stressful effort and reactivity, as well as of any
tendency to avoid the workplay of spiritual growth, so as to fall
into the effectiveness of equanimity, and to enjoy the serenity that
is within us. We dance on the path of awareness, which is
experiential and existential. Our once cherished moralizing
ideologies and our weighty metaphysical belief systems vaporize
in their irrelevance. We dance lightly but with the joyous fullness
of our being. Once committed to the strengthening and refining
of our egotism, and to the accomplishment of making better
judgments about things, we dwell in the lifeforce of our own
Compassionate Witness. We now long only to fade away into the

joyful bliss of being what we truly are—a pulsation in the dancing diaphragm of the universe. We become profoundly happy.

As we come to know in our hearts that we are a pulse in the dancing of Holy Spirit, we come to enjoy life thoroughly and authentically. We find ourselves living naturally and ethically— revering life, respecting belongingness, celebrating passion, expressing truthfulness, and honoring the temple of the bodymind.

The emptiness into which meditation casts us is ecstatic not only in the sense that it moves us out of the repetitious stasis in which our egotism is compulsively stuck. It is also ecstatic in the sense that it casts us into joy and bliss. In meditation, we access the lifeforce, the erotic energy that infuses everything that is and is not—and what is revealed here-and-now is the supreme truthfulness that the ecstatic emptiness of the lifeforce is Holy Spirit. It is the Sacred Unity of Love.

## The Pathless Path

Living in meditation liberates us from all that keeps us tethered, releasing us from our imprisonment in convention, repetition, and alienation. It moves us from the identitarian world of representations, into the experience of our existence as founded on an absolute emptiness that is the realization of Love. It moves us out of strategizing, out of the preoccupation with domination, possession and control, which characterize the imperial functioning of our egotism—as the conquistador that, in its delusions, it wishes it were. It moves us instead into the timespace of serenity and equanimity—and we find ourselves where we always already were on life's path of compassion, appreciation and grace.

Living in meditation is the prayerful cultivation of an exquisite awareness of the flow of the lifeforce within us, through us, and all around us. We come to realize that this is the supreme flow of emptying, which pervades all being and nonbeing. We come to realize our authentic, spontaneous, and natural being-in-the-world precisely as our egotism dissolves into our witnessing. We come to embrace our inherent deathfulness, and thus to celebrate life in all its joy, bliss, and ecstasy.

As we come to live in meditation, our egotism dissolves, our chattering mind is stilled, and we experience happiness beyond our wildest dreams. A mystical insight is given to us through meditation, an esoteric insight beyond anything our chattering mind could formulate: Ecstatic emptiness pervades all, is the sourcing of all, and is that Sacred Unity of Love, which is the supreme vibration of the universe.

Through this dancing passage is our enlightening. It is both gradual and immediate. It is a process of falling into the joy, bliss, and ecstasy that are present here-and-now. There is no destination to be established, no technique to be mastered, no authority to be obeyed—except for the inner promptings of our heart. The Sacred Unity of Love is truthfully the supreme flow of the universe. We are called to prayer. But this is not prayer as the petitioning or the praising of some other entity. Rather, it is prayer as the dancing that aligns us with the erotic energies of Holy Spirit, which pervades all that is and is not. Prayerfulness is our breathing, moving, dancing, vibrating, lovemaking and orgasming our way through life. This is the tantric way—the way of the *"BodyPrayerPath."*

Living in meditation is living in dancing prayer, and our hearts call us to live prayerfully. We are called to cast aside our egotism, and to cast our bodymind into prayerful alignment with the Sacred Unity of the lifeforce, which is Love. We are called to worship with the entirety of our erotic energies, to get "out of our heads" and into the sensuality of our genitals, our bodymind, and our hearts—to align our erotic lifeforce and our awareness of the lifeforce as Holy Spirit that it *is*.

Only living in the prayerfulness of meditation will free us from our imprisonment in all the suffering that is caused by human malice. For meditation is natural, spontaneous, sensual, and ethical—enabling us to participate joyfully even in life's hardship, pain and loss. Only living in the prayerfulness of meditation will bring us into the happiness that comes with a life of compassion, appreciation, and grace. For meditation celebrates life, and living in meditation we find ourselves, and everything around us, as fleeting as it may be and as harsh as it sometimes is, to be blessed with an infinite and eternal beauty. This essay came in appreciation of Osho's teachings, so it is now apt to quote his words:

*Meditation is your birthright!*
*It is there, waiting for you to relax a little so it can sing a song, become a dance . . .*
*Meditation is just to be . . . You are, and it is a sheer delight!*
*From where does this delight come?*
*It comes from nowhere, or it comes from everywhere.*
*It is uncaused, because existence is made of the stuff called joy.*

# ABOUT THE AUTHOR

 Trained as a psychoanalyst, sexuality educator and sex therapist, Barnaby B. Barratt has been involved in tantric spirituality for well over thirty years. Barnaby earned doctoral degrees in Psychology and Social Relations from Harvard University, and in Clinical and Educational Sexology from the Institute for Advanced Study of Human Sexuality. He completed postdoctoral research at the University of Michigan's Neuropsychiatric Institute, held the position of Professor of Family Medicine, Psychiatry and Behavioral Neurosciences for several years, and was elected to the Presidency of the American Association of Sexuality Educators, Counselors and Therapists. Barnaby currently devotes himself to the healing and celebrating practices of the *BodyPrayerPath*. He may be contacted through *www.BodyPrayerPath.org*.

BVG